HAJJ AND UMRAH

INNER DIMENSIONS TO THE JOURNEY OF LOVE

SHAYKH HUMAYUN HANIF MUJADDIDI

HAJJ AND UMRAH

INNER DIMENSIONS TO THE JOURNEY OF LOVE

Second Edition: 2022
Publisher: Maktaba Islahenafs, Karachi, Pakistan
www.islahenafs.org
Email: info@islahenafs.org
Phone: +92 321 2172484

AVAILABLE IN PAKISTAN

MAKTABA ISLAHENAFS
Phone: +92 321 2172484

DARUL ISHAAT
Phone: +92 21 32213786

AVAILABLE ON AMAZON

USA & CANADA, UNITED KINGDOM
AUSTRALIA, FRANCE, ITALY, SWEDEN, NETHERLANDS,
POLAND, SPAIN, DENMARK

ALSO AVAILABLE IN USA & CANADA

Ha-Meem Store
www.hameemstore.com
Phone: +1 416 8792545

Special thanks to my Shaykh Mowlana Shamsur Rehman Al Abbasi with whose dua, support and guidance this work has been compiled. Special thanks to all the scholars, whose literary work is cited. May Allah shower His blessings upon them. Due consideration is taken to cite the work.

All rights reserved by Maktaba Islahenafs, aside from fair use, meaning a few pages or less for non-profit educational purposes, review, or scholarly citation. No part of this publication maybe reproduced, stored in a retrieval system or transmitted in any form or means, electronic, online, mechanical, photocopying, recording or otherwise, without the prior permission of the copyright owner.

All Fiqh or Islamic jurisprudence rules regarding Hajj and Umrah are written by Mawlana Mufti Abdul Hameed Nakhuda, Naib Mufti Dar ul Iftáa at Jamia ul Uloom al Islamia, Binori Town, Karachi

Contents

About the Author 1

INNER STATE 5
Sincerity in Action 6

Deeds will not be Counted 12

Inner State 13

Intention 19

Preparation for the Journey 21

Take the Sound Heart 22

Gratitude for the Beloved Prophet ﷺ 23

Tests and Trials 26

Eyes on the Prize 28

INNER DIMENSIONS 31
Ihram 31

The First Sight 32

Circumambulation-Tawaf 34

The Black Stone-Hajr-e-Aswad 37

Sáe 38

Hajj 39

Arafat 44

Ramy 45

Sacrificing the Animal-Hady 46

Death upon Faith 47

VISITING MADINAH THE RADIANT 48
Entering Madinah the Radiant 51

Visiting the Masjid 53

Visiting the Rawdah	55
Journey Homewards	60
UMRAH	**61**
Miqat	62
Wearing the Ihram	65
Rules for Entering Miqat	68
Circumambulation-Tawaf	69
Istilam	69
Ramal	72
Sáe	72
Shaving and Trimming Hair-Halq and Taqsir	74
HAJJ	**76**
Obligatory Actions-Fard	77
Obligations-Wajib	77
Sunnah	78
Eighth Dhul Hijjah	79
Ninth Dhul Hijjah	79
Tenth Dhul Hijjah	80
Eleventh Dhul Hijjah	84
Twelfth Dhul Hijjah	85
Farewell Tawaf	85
TRANSGRESSIONS AND PENALTIES	**87**
Badanah	87
Damm	87
Sadaqah	88
VIOLATION OF IHRAM	**88**
Entering Miqat	88

Fragrance 89

Wearing Stitched Clothing (For Men) 91

Footwear 93

Covering the Head / Face 93

Shaving, Cutting & Removing Hair 93

Clipping the Nails 94

Sexual Relations 95

VIOLATION OF THE RITES 97

Tawaf al-Qudum 98

Tawaf al-Nafl 99

Tawaf al-Ziyarah 99

Tawaf al-Wida 101

Sáe of Hajj and Umrah 101

Mina 102

Day of Arafat 102

Night of Muzdalfah 103

Rami 103

VIOLATION OF THE HARAM 105

Hunting 105

Cutting Vegetation 107

SUPPLICATIONS 108

Before starting the journey 108

Upon leaving the house 111

Upon riding your vehicle 112

Upon feeling anxious 113

Upon entering Makkah or Madinah 114

Intention for Umrah 115

Entering the boundaries of Haram 116

At the entrance of the Haram 116

In the middle of the Haram 117

Intention of Iítikaaf 117

At the first sight upon Kaába 117

Intention for circumambulation (Tawaf) for Umrah 118

Intention for Tawaf al-Nafl 118

Standing in front of the Hajr e Aswad 118

Between Hajr e Aswad and Rukn e Shami, (first to third corner) 119

Between Rukn e Shami and Rukn e Yemeni (Third to fourth corner) 119

Between Rukn e Yemeni and Hajr e Aswad (fourth to first corner) 120

At Multazam 121

At Maqam e Ibraheem 122

Upon drinking Zamzam 122

Upon leaving from Baab al-Safa 123

Walking towards the Mount of Safa 123

Intention to make Saé 123

At Safa	124

Hajj 125

Intention for Hajj	125
From the Fajr of 9th Dhul Hijjah to Asar of 13th Dhul Hijjah	125
While in Arafat	125
Upon picking the pebbles at Muzdalfa	127
Upon casting pebbles at Shaytan	127

Supplications in Madinah-The Radiant 128

Upon the first sight of Madinah	128
Upon entering the Masjid al-Nabawi	128
Send Blessings upon the Beloved Prophet ﷺ	129
In front of the Sacred Rawdah	129
Sending blessings from someone else	131
Sending blessings from many people	131
Blessings upon Sayeddina Abu Bakr Siddique ؓ	131
Blessings upon Sayeddina Umar ؓ	132
Blessings to Sayeddina Abu Bakr Siddique ؓ and Sayeddina Umar ؓ	132
Upon visiting Jannat al-Baqeé	132
During the return journey	133
Upon reaching hometown	133
Upon reaching Home	134

About the Author

The author of the book, Shaykh Mohammad Ali Humayun Hanif Naqshbandi Mujaddidi is an accomplished author and a philanthropist. He has been a patron and amongst the Board of Governors for Liaquat National Hospital in Karachi and many other organisations. In 1989, Shaykh Mohammad Ali Humayun Hanif started attending Dhikr gatherings conducted by Hazrat Mawlana Shamsur Rehman Al Abbasi who further nurtured his yearning for the Love of Allah. In 1991, Hazrat Shaykh Mohammad Ali Humayun Hanif entered into Bayá (oath) with Mawlana Shamsur Rehman Al Abbasi. By the Grace of Allah ﷻ, in 1994, Hazrat Mawlana Shamsur Rehman Al Abbasi authorised him as a Shaykh. Shaykh Humayun Hanif was appointed as the first *Khalifa* (spiritual successor) of Mawlana Shamsur Rehman Al Abbasi and he gave '*ijazah*' (permission) to conduct *Dhikr* gatherings and guide others.

He has travelled widely across the globe and spent time in the company of many renowned scholars and *Awliya*. Shaykh Mohammad Ali Humayun Hanif is also authorised by Dr. Ismail Memon Madni; Khalifa of Shaykh al-Hadith Mawlana Mohammad Zakariya Kandhalvi ﷺ in

Naqshbandia, *Chistiya*, *Qadiriya* and *Soharwardiya* Orders. Mawlana Ishaq Sajid, Khalifa of Mawlana Ali Murtaza ؓ of Gadei Shareef also authorised Shaykh Mohammad Ali Humayun Hanif in the *Naqshbandia*, *Chistiya*, *Qadiriya*, *Soharwardiya and Shadhiliya* Orders.

Shaykh Humayun Hanif's vision is to purify and connect the individuals to Allah ﷻ by following the path of His Last Prophet ﷺ. He corroborates Islam as a *Deen*; a way of life and not just a set of rituals. Through his own practical example, he demonstrates to follow Shariáh, encompassing faith and action, behaviour, and morals, bringing together the practical and the spiritual aspects of human life as determined by Allah's Messenger ﷺ. Shaykh Humayun Hanif emphasises upon his students to become 'Active Muslims', both in their spiritual life and worldly matters. To achieve the desired outcome in the seekers, weekly *Dhikr* gatherings and lectures on *Tasawwuf* are conducted at *Khanqah e Shamsia* located in Karachi, Pakistan.

Lectures Available:

You Tube: Islahenafs-Shaykh Humayun Hanif

Website: www.islahenafs.org.

Other Publications by the Author:

- Sufism: Misconceptions and the Reality [English, 2022]
- Umrah aur Hajj- Ishq se Qurb ka Safar [Urdu, 2022]
- Duroos Maktoobat vol:I-Imam Rabbani Mujaddid Alf Thani ﷺ [Urdu, 2021]
- Ramadan kese Guzaren [Urdu, 2022]

Publications Under the Tutelage of the Author:

- Jamal e Mustafa ﷺ [Urdu, Published 2021]
- Rehmatul lil Alameen: Seerah of the Last Prophet Muhammad ﷺ [English, 2022]

4

INNER STATE

Hajj and Umrah is considered as a journey from one's abode to the House of Allah ﷻ. In true essence it is a migration from the carnal self towards Allah ﷻ. It is a journey that can ignite the soul to be reminded of the time it was created. It also takes the soul, beyond the dimensions of this life, to the time it will meet the Creator. Hajj is a set of rituals where the believer is intended to leave his ego and truly submit himself to the command of Allah ﷻ. From wearing an *Ihram* which comprises of two unstitched sheets to throwing pebbles at Shaytan, every ritual symbolises an action of absolute submission to Allah ﷻ.

Many people perform numerous Hajj and Umrah, yet they are unclear about the intention behind this great action. Some decide to take the journey as an opportunity for business, others may intend to fulfil their obligation. There are some who take the journey to be known by the title of *Haji* or take it as an opportunity for tourism. Whereas, the Prophet ﷺ supplicated:

> *"O Allah! (enable me to make) Hajj with no riya' (showing off with the desire that others witness one's good acts) or sumáh [showing off with the desire that others hear about one's good acts] in it." [Ibn Majah]*

Hajj and Umrah is supposed to be a life changing act for a believer; however, it so happens that we do perform Hajj and Umrah, yet our souls stay unaffected. According to a narration, *'at the end of the time, four classes of people will go on pilgrimage; their rulers for the outing; their rich men for trade; their poor for begging; their Qurán-readers for the benefit of their reputations.'* [Khatib, Sabuni]

We spend money, take time off our busy life styles, visit Makkah and Madinah and return home, oblivious of the real purpose for this journey. The question arises as to why even after performing the significant act of submission as Hajj and Umrah, our ways remain devious?

Sincerity in Action

Just as the body comprises of the material and the immaterial which is the physical body and the soul, there is an external aspect and an internal aspect of every action; the intention with which the deed is performed for whom it is performed and why is it performed. Soul does not need words, it has a silent language of its own, linked to the inner state of the heart which decides the destiny of a deed. Abu Umamah ؓ narrated that the Beloved Prophet ﷺ said,

"Allah said: The most beloved act with which my servant worships me is sincerity for my sake." [Ahmad]

For a deed to be accepted on the Day of Judgement, the criterion is;

❖ The deed must be the actions that Allah declared as good deeds,
❖ The deed must be performed according to the method outlined by Shariáh-the Islamic Jurisprudence,
❖ The deed must be done for Allah ﷻ.

Hajj and Umrah is definitely one of the actions Allah ﷻ declared as good deeds, which is performed according to the method outlined by Shariáh. The missing criteria is that 'the deed must be done purely for Allah'. It comes down to the intention and the sincerity of the action. The details of faith and action combined with the pure state of the heart have been explicitly shown to us by the Prophet ﷺ, through his own life, as an example. On the day of judgement, Allah will decide on the sincerity of the deed. Consider the first Hadith of Sahih Bukhari;

"The reward of the deeds depends upon the intention"
[Bukhari:1]

Hajj and Umrah is an act which demands complete submission to Allah ﷻ with the physical body and the spiritual heart. For the body it is in the acts of obedience in accordance with Shariáh and for the heart it is in the cognizance of Allah ﷻ and keeping the intention pure. The Messenger ﷺ said,

"The true emigrant is a person who leaves behind everything that Allah has forbidden" *[Bukhari: 6484, Abu Dawood:2481]*

It is evident from the Hadith that the true migrant is the one who abandons everything which Allah ﷻ has forbidden. Nonetheless, no one should assume from the Hadith that the outward practices of Islam are without value, in fact Allah ﷻ has created for every inner meaning an external form and without performing the external deed, the inner significance is impossible.

In Islam, the action and the deed are extremely important and the value to those deeds is added through the sincerity of intention. For every internal action there has to be an external action and the value in that external action is achieved by the internal aspect. As the body is nothing without a soul and a soul is immaterial without a body. Hence, the external or the outer aspect of the deed and the inner aspect of the deed are interrelated, an action only becomes an action in virtue of its sincerity.

Sincerity has the same relation to an action as the soul to the body. A body without a soul is called dead and an action without sincerity is worthless. It is the pure intention and the cognizance of Allah which gives the profound meaning to the good deed. Prayer or Salah for example, is not really Salah until performed with purification, intention (*Niyah*), direction towards *Qibla*; it is an action but if not performed with knowledge, it will lose its essence. As Quran mentions;

"Successful indeed are the believers; those who humble themselves in the prayers." [Quran, al-Múminun 23:1-2]

Another misconception undermining the deed and the action is that the intention should be pure and sincerity of the heart is enough. Some claim that they are very sincere in their heart, therefore, they do not need to perform any deed as per Shariáh because the deeds are just external actions. Remember, these are the people deceived by the devil and lost in the darkness as the internal aspect of an action cannot take place without its external counterpart. A man may keep his heart earnest throughout his entire life, yet there is no sincerity until it is combined with action. Similarly, a person may perform external actions throughout his life, his actions do not become acts of devotion until they are combined with sincerity. Consider the Hadith related in Muslim that:

"The first person judged on Resurrection Day will be a man martyred in battle. He will be brought forth, Allah ﷻ will reacquaint him with His blessings upon him and the man will acknowledge them, whereupon Allah ﷻ will say, "What have you done with them?". The man will respond, "I fought to the death for You."

Allah ﷻ will reply, "You lie. You fought in order to be called a hero, and it has already been said." Then, he will be sentenced and dragged away on his face and flung into the fire.

Next, a man will be brought forward who learnt the Sacred Knowledge, taught it to others and recited the Qur'an. Allah ﷻ will remind him of His gifts to him and the man will acknowledge them. Then, Allah ﷻ will say, "What have you done with them?" The man will answer, "I acquired Sacred Knowledge, taught it and recited the Qur'an, for Your sake."

Allah ﷻ will say, "You lie. You learnt so as to be called a scholar, read the Qur'an so as to be called a reciter, and it has already been said." Then, the man will be sentenced and dragged away on his face to be flung into the fire.

Next, a man will be brought forward whom Allah ﷻ generously provided for, giving him various kinds of wealth. Allah ﷻ will recall to him the benefits given and the man will acknowledge them, to which Allah ﷻ will say, "And what have you done with them?" The man will answer, "I have not left a single expense You love to see made, except that I have spent it for Your sake."

Allah ﷻ will say, "You lie. You did it so to be called generous, and it has already been said." Then, he will be sentenced and dragged away on his face to be flung into the fire. *[Muslim 1905]*

The Hadith gives an in depth understanding of the sincerity and the worth of intention behind a deed, even when one willingly gives away his life or his wealth. Without a pure and sincere intention, the deed is not accepted by Allah ﷻ. The scholar acquired and taught sacred knowledge, martyr gave his life and the altruistic gave his money but the intention was not pure so nothing was accepted.

Deeds will not be Counted

At times, we count the deeds and give a great importance to number. For example, one of us may flaunt about the number of Umrah or Hajj performed. It is a great blessing if someone gets to perform many Umrahs and Hajj, but at the same time we must try to perform these actions and deeds with utmost sincerity. It is mentioned in Qur'an that the deeds will be weighed not counted;

"..So, as for those whose scale (of good deeds) will be heavy, they will be the successful (by entering Paradise)" [Qurán, al-Aáraf 7:8]

The question then arises as to what brings the weight to the deeds? The rewards for the good deeds are only bestowed if the acts are purely for Allah ﷻ, not even for a reward in the afterlife. The deeds are to be performed selflessly without any interest in this world or the next. When the heart is purified of *riya*, Allah ﷻ discloses the reality and the servant is able to perform the acts of obedience in the true spirit.

When the act of obedience is done purely to draw closer to Allah ﷻ, no matter how small the act is, it becomes significant, as the Beloved Prophet ﷺ said, *"If one of you were to spend the weight of mount Uhud in gold, it would still not be equal to one of their [Companions' alms] bushel-weights or even half of that."* [Muslim 2540]

When the act of obedience is done purely with the intention to draw closer to Allah ﷻ, the Almighty not only accepts those but also accepts the rest even if deficient, as in Qurán;

"Whoever works righteous, man or woman, while believing, We shall certainly bestow them a life wondrous fair, and shall truly requite them their wage as if each deed were the best they ever did." [Qurán, an Nahl 16:97]

Inner State

The importance of inner state is clearly indicated as a part of a lengthy narration that the Beloved Prophet ﷺ said, *"For sure, it is not your bodies or forms which concern Allah, but your hearts and your deeds. Piety (Taqwa) is here! Piety is here! Piety is here!" And he pointed to his chest. [Bukhari, Muslim, Abu Dawud, Tirmidhi]*

Hajj and Umrah is an act of devotion where the pilgrim is required to utterly surrender in complete obedience to Allah. The actions of Hajj, such as abandonment of stitched clothing, Tawaf, Saé, the time in Arafat, stoning the Jamarat, and shaving the head do not have an obvious meaning. Each and every act is a show of complete surrender to the will and the command of Allah. The Beloved Prophet ﷺ said,

"The reward for Accepted Hajj (Mabroor) is nothing else but Jannah." [Bukhari]

The evidence of accepted Hajj is steadfastness of the servant after Hajj in practicing righteous acts and abstinence from sins. Hasan al-Basri ﷜ defined the concept as, "An accepted Hajj is to return abstinent from this world and desiring the Hereafter. As Allah mentions in Qurán: *"And those who are guided-He increases them in guidance and gives them their righteousness." [Qurán, Muhammad 47:17]" [Mirat-ul-Manajih, vol. 5, pp. 441; Fath-ul-Baari, vol. 4, pp. 329, Taht-al-Hadees: 1521]*

Regarding an accepted Hajj, Imam Ghazali رَحْمَةُ اللهِ عَلَيْهِ wrote, "If a person suffers a loss or physical or financial trouble, he should accept it contentedly, abstain from sins, avoid evil company and keep the company of the pious. The person should avoid heedlessness and join the gatherings of Dhikr. Upon his return, a person should become uninterested in worldly matters and pay attention to the matters regarding Hereafter; and after beholding *Baytullah* he should prepare for meeting his Lord.

One indication that the Hajj or Umrah is accepted is that when a pilgrim abandons his sinful ways, exchanging his idle companions for the righteous company and forsaking haunts of heedlessness and frivolity in exchange for gatherings of Remembrance of Allah ﷻ." *[Ihya-ul-'Uloom, vol. 1, pp. 349-354]*

It is narrated that Abdullah bin Mubarak رَحْمَةُ اللهِ عَلَيْهِ went to Makkah to perform Hajj. One night, while he was sleeping near Kaába, in his dream, he saw two angels descend from the sky. One of the angels asked the other: "I wonder if anyone's Hajj has been accepted?"

The second replied, "There is a man in Damascus but he could not come for Hajj. Allah ﷻ has accepted his intention of Hajj and because of him Allah ﷻ accepted all these pilgrims and rewarded them."

Abdullah bin Mubarak ﵀ was surprised and decided to find the man whose intention was so pure that Allah accepted all the pilgrims. He went to Damascus and asked people if they knew anyone who intended to go for Hajj and was left behind. He was directed to a blacksmith who had prepared for the journey but did not go for Hajj. Abdullah bin Mubarak went to see him and asked him as to why he did not perform Hajj as planned. The man replied "For thirty years I have lived in the hope of performing the Hajj. Finally, I had saved enough, but Allah did not will it and that is why I could not go for Hajj."

Abdullah bin Mubarak ﵀ was curious to find out how the man's Hajj was accepted and blessed for all the people who went for Hajj, even when he himself did not perform Hajj. Abdullah bin Mubarak ﵀ asked the man again as to why he could not go for Hajj, still the man gave a simple reply. When Abdullah bin Mubarak ﵀ persisted and told him about his dream. The man revealed: "My neighbour cooked something which my child insisted upon eating. My neighbour's family ate while he did not extend the courtesy. I found it odd and asked him. He was very embarrassed and told me that the food was prepared from a dead animal as his family had been starving for many days. The food was permitted for him but not for us, therefore he did not offer us any."

The man continued, "Upon knowing about my neighbour's suffering, I gave all my savings to him as I thought I could not bear to go for Hajj leaving him in such a miserable state. Although, I still desire to go for Hajj, if Allah wills."

At times, most of us who plan to take the journey are unaware of the importance of intention. Some will visit Makkah to fulfil an obligation, others may perform the Hajj to be called Haji. Same goes for Umrah, there are those who just take it as a business opportunity or a holiday. If you ask one of the returning pilgrims about their journey, most likely the reply would be; "It was very comfortable, the travel, the accommodation and the meals everything was quite nice." Mostly, the answer would be regarding the physical aspects, not the inner aspects of this great journey.

Most of us return home without any change in our lives. A close friend, Abid Binnori used to work for Saudi Airline. He said there was a time when people would embark the plane with tearful eyes, invoking *Labbaik Allahuma Labbaik*, now you see the pilgrims leisurely chewing gum, as if going for a holiday. Is this journey really insignificant or the reality of Kaába has changed over time? The truth is that nothing has changed except for our intentions and our understanding of this journey. There is no change in Allah's Benevolence, it is still the same, however, we have no idea what this journey truly demands and the objective of Hajj and Umrah.

Hajj and Umrah begin with understanding the significance of these actions in Islam. From yearning, to wearing an Ihram to standing in Arafat, each and every ritual is a reminder of total submission to Allah ﷻ. The members of earlier religious communities asked the Messenger ﷺ, if the ways of the monks and anchorites were followed in Islam. The Messenger ﷺ replied, *"Allah has replaced them for us with the Jihad and the declaration of His supremacy on every elevated place (alluding to Hajj)"* [Bayhaqi]

Allah ﷻ has favoured the Muslims by making Hajj its form of monasticism and has honoured Kaába as His own. Allah ﷻ has dignified the sanctity of the place by declaring its game and trees inviolate. The believers come to the Sacred city from every deep ravine and every distant scene, dishevelled, dusty and humble to show their total submission. Human brain is unable to rationalise the significance of the rituals and action as stoning the pillars, and running back and forth in Saé, but they demonstrate the perfection of a believer's submission to Allah ﷻ. The sole purpose to perform these rituals and actions is the Command itself and the intention to comply. The performance of these inexplicable duties is a form of devotion most effective in purifying the soul with the condition that the intention be sincere and pure. Therefore, before even taking this journey, one must seek the right intention.

Intention

When we prepare for a journey, we plan the travel itinerary, accommodation etc. Even for this special journey, we are mostly concerned about hotel accommodation, flights, clothes and meals. There is no harm in planning and preparing for a comfortable journey but this should not take over the essence of this journey and become a priority.

The Beloved Prophet ﷺ used to pray for the blessings of Ramadan from the start of the month of Rajab, which is two months before Ramadan.

Similarly, the preparations for this journey should start well in advance. The time which it would take for the travelling agent to get the documents organised is a critical time for the pilgrim too. This is the time for the pilgrim to start thinking about being presented in *Baytullah* which Allah ﷻ calls as His House.

Allah ﷻ is with us wherever we are, but Kaába is a special place in terms of Allah's Manifestations and Madinah the Radiant is the city of the Beloved Prophet ﷺ. To visit these Sacred places special preparation is required. To achieve the true purpose of Hajj and Umrah, it is vital to have the right intention. If one intends to perform the Hajj or Umrah with an intention of reward and blessings, he would definitely receive that. However, if he performs the same Hajj or Umrah with an intention of love, he would achieve Allah's *rida* or pleasure and still be rewarded with blessings. Therefore, even before the planning phase, one must clearly think and assign the true intention to this journey. The intention should be to achieve Allah's ﷻ pleasure and proximity. The resolve should be purely for Allah ﷻ, untarnished by hypocrisy and desire for fame as there is nothing more shameful than to visit the House of Allah ﷻ for ulterior motive. If the intention is sincere the action will be accepted.

Preparation for the Journey

We become more concerned about the physical aspects of the journey as how many pairs of shoes and sets of clothing to pack. However, this is not an ordinary journey, it is a journey of love from the carnal self to the Creator. With the pure and sincere intention to achieve Allah's pleasure, one has to cleanse the filth of sins accumulated over the soul during the course of ordinary life.

Allah's Messenger ﷺ said, *"Whenever a servant commits an act of wrongdoing, a black spot appears on his heart and when he desists, and seeks forgiveness, and repents, his heart will become clear. But, if he again commits the same wrongs, more and more black marks will accumulate until they overshadow his heart. This is the rust which the Almighty speaks of in the Qur'an [Qur'an, 83:4]"* [Tirmidhi: 3334, Ibn Majah: 4244]

As the Beloved Prophet ﷺ said, "..seek forgiveness and repent", which will clear the heart. For the believer who repents, Allah ﷻ gives the glad tidings in Qurán:

"Whoever commits evil or wrongs themselves then seeks Allah's forgiveness will certainly find Allah All-Forgiving, Most Merciful." [*Qurán, An Nisa 4:110*]

One should continue performing the Salah for repentance every day and seek forgiveness from Allah ﷻ for all the sins. Start excessive recitation of *Salawat* or durood shareef which is considered a fragrance for the soul. Make a pledge to abstain from any sin may it be minor or major, repent to Allah ﷻ and sever the heart's connection with what is behind you.

Take the Sound Heart

Kaába is a place of special significance; A believer can perform Salah, recite Qurán or any other righteous deed anywhere in the world but Tawaf or circumambulation of Kaába cannot be done elsewhere. When the believer gets to visit *Baytullah*, one should appreciate and recognise the blessing he has been accorded by Allah ﷻ. Allah neither looks at the appearance nor knowledge or status. Allah ﷻ asks the believers to present a sound heart, for this Qurán mentions the term Qalb e Saleem;

'When he came to His Lord with a sound heart' [*Qurán, As Saafat 37:84*]

In another verse, Qurán mentions;

"The Day when there will be no benefit from wealth or sons, but only one who comes to Allah with a pure heart."
[Qurán, Ash Shuára 26:88-89]

According to scholars as Ibn e Abbas؄, Ibne Sireen ؄ and al Alusi ؄, *'Qalb e Saleem'* is a pure heart free from disbelief, hypocrisy, pride or jealousy, filled with faith and sincerity. The believer is to bring Qalb e Saleem on the Day of Judgement and for that purpose the heart is to be prepared in this world free from disbelief, hypocrisy and pride. When one presents himself to *Baytullah* meaning the House of Allah ؄, one should prepare to take Qalb e Saleem.

Gratitude for the Beloved Prophet ﷺ

Once you plan the journey, start sending *Salawat* (reciting Durood Shareef) in abundance. This should be the gift you should take to Madinah, the Radiant city of the Beloved Prophet ﷺ. The Beloved Prophet ﷺ does not need our *Salawat* or benediction, it is just to show our own gratitude towards him. Allah ؄ has promised him the highest Station of praise and glory; *Maqam e Mahmood*, as mentioned in Qurán:

> *"Your Lord will raise to a station of great glory (Maqam e Mahmood)"* [Qurán, Al Israá 17:79]

Sending *Salawat* is symbolic to show our gratitude for him as we are indebted to the Beloved Prophet ﷺ till eternity. Sending salutations or *Salawat* is an expression of love for the Beloved Prophet ﷺ, while obtaining Allah's ﷻ love. Through Durood or *Salawat*, we seek closeness to Allah by acknowledging His favours and adhering to the command of Allah ﷻ as mentioned in Qurán:

> *"Allah and His angels send Salawat on the Prophet s.a.w: O you who believe! Send your Salawat upon him and salute him with all respect"* [Qurán, Al Ahzab, 33:56]

The Beloved Prophet ﷺ is neither in need of our Durood nor does it benefit him, in fact, we are the actual beneficiaries of Salawat or Durood, as mentioned in Hadith, the Beloved Prophet ﷺ said, *"Whoever sends Salawat upon me once, will be blessed by it tenfold, erased by it ten sins, and raised by it ten degrees in status"* [Sunan An-Nasa'i]

The Beloved Prophet ﷺ made innumerable sacrifices for us and placed us before his own self. Although our eyes have never seen the Beloved Prophet ﷺ, yet our hearts yearn his proximity.

Sending the *Salawat* increases our love for the Beloved Prophet ﷺ and through love, our heart connects with the Beloved Prophet ﷺ. The one who sends *Salawat* in abundance is freed from the worries of the worldly affairs as narrated by Ubay ibn Káab ؓ that he asked the Beloved Prophet ﷺ, "O Allah's Messenger ﷺ! I frequently invoke Allah to send Salawat upon you. How much of my supplication should I devote to you (*Salawat*)?" He said, "You may devote as much as you wish."

When I suggested "a quarter", he said, "Do whatever you wish, but it will be better for you if you increase it." I suggested "a half", he replied, "Do whatever you wish, but it will be better for you if you increase it." I suggested "two-thirds", he then said, "Do whatever you wish, but it will be better for you if you increase it." I said, "Shall I devote all my supplications to send *Salawat* upon you?"

He said, "Then you will be freed from your worries and your sins will be forgiven." *[Sunan At-Tirmizi]*

The other benefit of sending Salawat is that it purifies the heart as the Beloved Prophet ﷺ said, *"Send the Salawat upon me, for verily it is a purification for you."* *[Musnad Ahmad]*

It is narrated by Sayyedina Umar Ibn Al-Khattab ؓ said, "Indeed the supplication stops between the Heavens and the earth. Nothing of it is raised up until you send *Salawat* upon your Prophet ﷺ." [Sunan At-Tirmizi]

In fact, the Beloved Prophet ﷺ taught us how to make Dua as mentioned in Hadith, *"When any of you prays, let him begin by praising Allah ﷻ, then let him send blessings upon the Prophet ﷺ, then let him ask for whatever he wants."* [Sunan At-Tirmizi]

Tests and Trials

There were times when pilgrims used to take the journey on foot, camels or even boats. The extraordinary trials and hardships they faced to reach *Baytullah* are unimaginable. We do not have to walk for hundreds of miles through the sandy desert or the treacherous terrain, neither do we have to sail on a boat for months on the rough sea to reach Makkah. With technological advancement and modern way of commute, our travel is much faster, convenient and comfortable. Therefore, you need to understand that it is a journey of love where you are going to behold the sight of the Beloved from your heart. Every hurdle you cross brings you one step closer to your Beloved.

This is a journey in pursuit of Allah ﷻ and each and every step taken will be rewarded and bring one closer to the Beloved. There would be times when one's patience would be tested by waiting in long queues or standing in the heat. Just remind yourself the purpose of this journey and stay calm. The time you spend waiting at the airport or waiting for your bus, is not wasted, it is still counted towards your journey towards Allah ﷻ. Even if someone dies during this journey, the Beloved Prophet ﷺ said, *"If someone sets out from his home as a pilgrim or visitant (mútamir) and then dies, he is granted the reward of a pilgrim or visitant till the Day of Resurrection. Anyone who dies in either of the Sanctuaries (Makkah or Madinah) is not subject to review or reckoning, but is told to enter Paradise."* [Bayhaqi]

You should deal with good conduct, which means putting up with difficult situations. They say that the Arabic word for 'journey' is *safar*, because it reveals (*yusifiruán*) a person's character. Umar ؓ asked someone who claimed to know a man, 'Have you accompanied him on a journey?" Since the answer was no, he told him, 'Then, I don't see how you can know him!'

Eyes on the Prize

Throughout this journey, stay focused on your own actions, deeds and thoughts. Avoid criticizing or picking at others. Leave others to their own and mind your own business. You are not there to criticize others, rather the objective of your journey is to find Allah's *rida* or pleasure. If you criticize your Muslim brother, that would be detrimental to your own journey. There is a parable that Qays or as some call him Majnun was in love with Layla. Once, he was deeply engrossed in his own thoughts and crossed before a person who was performing Salah. The man was annoyed, so Qays said to him, 'I beg your pardon, I was engrossed in the thoughts of my beloved Layla. Although, it was my worldly love which made me aloof from my surroundings, but you were presented before the Lord, and you were still aware of your surroundings!'

Do not get distracted by what others are doing, just stay focused and calm. Continue with your supplications and do not waste your breath criticizing others. This is a place where supplications are accepted and calls answered. According to a Hadith, the Beloved Prophet ﷺ said, *'Pilgrims and visitors are the emissaries and visitors of Allah ﷻ; if they petition Him, He gives what they ask, if they seek His forgiveness, He forgives them, if they call on Him, He answers and if they seek intercession, it is granted." [Ibne Maja]*

This journey is for the sake of Allah ﷻ, the objective is neither worldly gains, nor riches. When the Beloved Prophet ﷺ called the disbelievers to Islam and said to them, "Say no one is God except Allah and then you will succeed." Consider the words of our Beloved Prophet Muhammad ﷺ, when the disbelievers came to his uncle Abu Talib and asked, 'What does your nephew want out of his call to Islam? If he wants status, we will give him status and we will not do anything without his consultation. If he wants money, we will give him money, until he becomes the richest amongst us. If he wants to rule us, we shall give him the position of king.' The Beloved Prophet ﷺ said to his uncle, 'If they were to place the sun in my right hand and the moon in my left, I would not leave this call to Islam.' The Beloved Prophet's ﷺ statement is the testament of his love for Allah ﷻ.

As a pilgrim, you are one amongst the billions who have been accorded the blessing to visit the Sacred House. Amongst billions of others Allah ﷻ has chosen you to be presented in Baytullah. It is a great blessing, so beware of your status and show gratitude. The reward of this journey is the love of Allah ﷻ which is a blessing incomparable to any other. Keep your heart engaged in the remembrance of Allah ﷻ, keep the worldly desires aside and realise that you have landed on the land most Sacred on earth. Therefore, feel privileged to be in the city chosen by Allah ﷻ to be the most Sacred place.

INNER DIMENSIONS

Ihram

The two seamless garments are symbolic to the shroud, reminding one of the meeting with his Lord. All dressed alike, the rich and the poor, the weak and the strong, this is when one should rid the carnal self from 'Me, mine and I'. The moment when you call *Talbiya or Labbayk* is a moment when you respond to the summons of Allah ﷻ as Allah ﷻ mentions in Qurán;

'And proclaim the pilgrimage among men.' [Qurán, al Hajj, 22:27]

It is an attire to show complete humility; everyone wearing the same garb without any pockets, looking alike. The believer takes off his clothes, reminding himself of the Day of judgement and presents before Allah ﷻ in the most humble state. It is important to rid your carnal self from the worldly status and everything which is attached to this world and presents before Allah ﷻ in the purest state. Supplicate and show humility and say, 'Allah ﷻ, I am presenting myself to you, sinful, destitute and bereft, seeking only You, my Lord!'

The First Sight

If you are in Makkah with an intention for an Umrah, ensure that you do not perform Umrah if you are exhausted from your travel. Even if you are wearing Ihram, you should have some rest before you take up the rituals. If you are tired, you will not be able to focus and all the rituals will be performed inattentively. If needed, take a quick nap to feel fresh, then go to Kaába.

When you first see Kaába, the heart should be conscious and the eyes should venerate it seeming to behold the sight of the Beloved. Do not hasten, take your time and cherish the moments. Envisage the Divine Manifestations upon Kaába, which are the true essence of the Sacred House. It is not the walls or the stones that we face when we perform Salah, we face those Divine Manifestations that are presented to Kaába. You are in a place, which is Sacred and Allah ﷻ has given it a special status, Allah ﷻ has accorded you to visit this place and His bounties are infinite. According to Ibne Abbas ؓ, the Beloved Prophet ﷺ said, *'One hundred and twenty mercies descend upon this House each day; sixty for those performing Tawaf, forty for those performing prayers and twenty for those who just look at it."* [Bayhaqi]

As you would be aware, that Allah ﷻ grants whatever one beseeches upon the first sight. Do not worry, if the eyes blink, stay focused, as the treasures and blessings of Allah ﷻ are not limited to the blink of an eye. Communication is not limited to words, with heart absorbed by the True Reality, eyes shedding tears of repentance, beseech Allah ﷻ as if you see Him. In these precious moments, just use your own emotions to express rather than reciting the supplications from a book, unless you have memorized those. If you would try to recite the supplications from a book, your attention would be diverted and your own feelings and emotions will not be expressed. When a lover is in the presence of the Beloved, words become meaningless and emotions are expressed by tears. Annihilate yourself in the Divine and beseech, 'Allah ﷻ I am nothing and I have nothing, only that I am your slave and You are my Lord and I am from the nation of Your Beloved Prophet ﷺ.'

Seek everything you desire for your own self, your family, friends and the whole Ummah. Plead with your heart and soul, beg Allah ﷻ to grant you from His infinite bounties and blessings. Beseech Allah

ﷻ to grant you His vision, His Noble countenance in the Hereafter just as He has granted you the vision of his House. Plead to Allah ﷻ to include you in the company of those who reach him. As one of our elders said, "Seek Allah ﷻ from Allah ﷻ for Allah ﷻ."

Circumambulation-Tawaf

It is narrated that the Beloved Prophet ﷺ said, *"Make frequent circuits of the House, for this will be among the glories of your records on the Day of Resurrection, and the most fortunate action credited to you."* [Hakim]

This is the action where the believer goes around the Manifestations of the Lord in circles, showing his humility, reverence and ultimate love. Again, imagine amongst billions, you have been chosen to be in the Sacred city, in the Sacred House, performing Tawaf. Many more may have been in the Sacred city or even in Masjid al-Haram, but you are amongst those who are circumambulating Kaába just like angels around the Throne. Tawaf on its own is such a commendable act that according to Hadith, *"To circuit seven times, barefoot or bareheaded, is as meritorious as freeing a slave, while he who performs Tawaf*

seven times in the rain is forgiven all his previous sins."
[Tirmidhi]

Fill your heart with reverence, fear, hope and love. As Imam Ghazali ﷺ said, know that in Tawaf, you resemble the angels near the Divine Presence, who ring the Throne and circle around it. The purpose of Tawaf is not just circumambulation of the Sacred House, rather your heart should be circling in the remembrance of the Lord of the House. There are seventy thousand angels who perform Tawaf of Bayt al Mámur which is just above Kaába and corresponds to Kaába in the Heavens. Those angels who perform Tawaf once, never get a chance again and this is Allah's Benevolence that He has accorded you to perform Tawaf in the wake of those angels. For those who seek Him, Allah ﷻ removes the boundaries of the physical and the invisible world. Allah ﷻ is not in need of anything, as mentioned in Qurán:

"O humanity! It is you who stand in need of Allah, but Allah ˹alone˺ is the Self-Sufficient, Praiseworthy." [Qurán, Fatir 35:15]

Yet, Allah ﷻ the Merciful and the Most Benevolent grants us the Bounties and the Blessings when we beseech and accepts our repentance when we seek forgiveness. During Tawaf, praise Allah ﷻ and seek forgiveness. Seek forgiveness for everyone, even your enemies. When the pilgrim seeks forgiveness for someone else, Allah ﷻ forgives him and the person for whom he seeks forgiveness, as the Beloved Prophet ﷺ supplicated to Allah ﷻ,

"O Allah ﷻ, Forgive the pilgrim and those for whom the pilgrim seeks forgiveness!" [Hakim]

When you seek forgiveness for others, you will be granted the supplication of the Beloved Prophet ﷺ. Beseech as if you see Allah's Countenance and although, He knows it all, share with Him all your worries, pains and troubles. You will be tired of begging, but Allah ﷻ will not be tired of giving. All the burdens of life will come off your shoulders, a sense of peace and tranquillity will overcome you. Your heart will be relieved of all the worries and filled with joy and peace.

Keep your caste down as it is not allowed to look at Kaába during Tawaf and complete each circuit as if you are circling around the Throne of Allah ﷻ. If you want to Praise Allah ﷻ or perform Dhikr, then recite *La ilaha illallah*, keeping in mind the true meaning of this verse. If you want to recite *Subhan Allah*, then truly Praise Him; not just mere words, but admire His True Beauty. There is no need for counting, just let the heart follow the Praise.

The Black Stone-Hajr-e-Aswad

According to Hadith, *"The Black stone is a ruby from Paradise. It will be raised on the Day of Judgement with a pair of eyes and a tongue to speak, testifying for all those who have touched it with truth and sincerity."* [Tirmidhi, Nisai]

When you gesture towards Hajr e Aswad which is termed as *istilam*, ensure to turn your heart towards Allah ﷻ and nullify any other thoughts. It is said that when one performs *istilam* or gestures towards the Black stone, the state of the heart is sealed. When you gesture towards the Black Stone, it is an allegiance to be obedient to Allah ﷻ, so stay firm on your resolve for the rest of your life.

Kissing the Black stone is Sunnah. If you can easily get the access then do perform this, Sunnah, but do not push or hurt others to get close to the Black Stone. Islam does not allow you to hurt your brother, as narrated by Ibn Abbas﷜, the Beloved Prophet ﷺ said,

"Be afraid, from the curse of the oppressed as there is no screen between his invocation and Allah." [Bukhari: 2448]

You are in *Baytullah* where prayers are answered, therefore, avoid pushing or hurting anyone, as you do not want the curse of the oppressed in the Sacred House. If you get pushed, forgive that person and seek Allah's forgiveness for that person and Allah ﷻ will grant you with His immense blessings.

Sáe

Saé is the running or walking between al-Safa and al-Marwa. Allah ﷻ mentioned this in Qurán as:

"Surely the Safa and the Marwa are among the signs appointed by Allah" [Qurán Al Baqara 2:158]

By the orders of Allah ﷻ, Ibraheem ؑ left his wife Hajira ؑ and his infant son Ismael ؑ in the barren valley of Makkah. This was a great test as hundreds of miles of barren land laid across with no water or shelter. When Ibraheem ؑ departed, she ran after him and asked him as to why he was leaving her behind. He was ordered not to say anything, Hajira ؑ then asked him, 'Are you leaving us by the orders of Allah?' To which he replied, 'Yes'. She then, said, 'Allah ﷻ is enough for us.' The little water she had, soon finished and the baby was crying. In her devastation to find water, she ran between the two hills. Her heart was melting by the wailing of her baby, yet she had a strong faith in Allah ﷻ and believed that help would arrive. Allah ﷻ sent His Angel Gibrael ﷺ, who touched the tip of his wing where Ismael ﷺ rubbed his feet and water gushed from the ground. This is how the water from Zamzam started.

Envision the desolate barren land, where a lonely mother was left with her baby and how she ran between the two hills in despair. When you run between Safá and Marwa, imagine that you are running towards Allah ﷻ. Seek Allah's Mercy as you go back and forth between Safá and Marwa as this is a place of Allah's immense Mercy.

Hajj

The vision of Allah's ﷻ Noble countenance will be accorded in the abode of eternity. The mortal eye is unfitted to behold the vision of Allah ﷻ in this world, but in the Hereafter, the human vision will be prepared to hold His Glorious Countenance. Meanwhile, when one takes the journey to the House of Allah ﷻ, the journey creates a longing for all that would lead to the meeting with Allah ﷻ as the lover yearns for anything connected to the Beloved.

Hajj is a set of rituals, which mind cannot comprehend and rationality does not play a role. These actions represent perfect demonstration of homage and obedience to the Command of the Creator. To carry out these Commands, the carnal self is deflected and brought to servitude. It is a journey towards the Creator and the Most Merciful, our Lord without any associates; Allah ﷻ. Our Lord loves us, even though He does not need us whereas, we need Him, yet we forget Him. Hajj is the journey of Love, where you need to involve your soul and heart with your physical self. This is why the Beloved Prophet ﷺ said,

> *"Doubly at Your service, through a pilgrimage in truth, devotion and homage!"* [al- Daraqutni]

The Beloved Prophet ﷺ said, *"(Allah says) O son of Adam, so long as you call upon Me and ask of Me, I shall forgive you for what you have done, and I shall not mind. O son of Adam, were your sins to reach the clouds of the sky and were you then to ask forgiveness of Me, I would forgive you. O son of Adam, were you to come to Me with sins nearly as great as the earth and were you then to face Me, ascribing no partner to Me, I would bring you forgiveness nearly as great as this."* [Tirmidhi]

Allah ﷻ has given Hajj as an opportunity for the believers to seek forgiveness and be granted with His Mercy. The Beloved Prophet ﷺ said, *"He who makes pilgrimage to the House, avoiding indecent and immoral behaviour, emerges from his sins like a newborn baby."* [Bukhari and Muslim]

If you have been given the honour to perform Hajj, do not consider it as an ordinary opportunity. It signifies Allah's ﷻ love and Mercy for you, as He has accorded you to visit the Sacred house which He calls as His own. This opportunity is significant and one cannot attain it on his own will. This is not about being rich or poor, young or old as there are many who can afford but never get the opportunity to perform Hajj. Yet, there are many who are poor but get this opportunity to perform Hajj. If Allah ﷻ has chosen you, then be grateful as He wishes to take you in His Rehma or Mercy. When you visit *Baytullah*, seek the Lord of the House, do not waste your time seeking worldly goods in the shopping centres, in case you return home with your hands full of shopping bags and an empty heart.

One of my brothers from Silsila or the spiritual chain is an extremely sincere and pious man. He had meagre resources, yet he went for Hajj every year. Few years ago, he came to me and said that he saw the Beloved Prophet ﷺ in his dream and that the Beloved Prophet ﷺ sent Salam and asked me to organise for his Hajj. I had no doubt in his statement, yet I was surprised. He was leaving to visit his family in the village but I did not have spare funds to pay for his Hajj travel. Nevertheless, I asked him to leave his passport and Hajj documents with me. In those days, the Hajj applications were submitted through the Banks along with the money.

Finally, the last date for submission of application arrived and still there was nothing I could do. I looked at the clock, the banks closed at 1.30 p.m. and it was already 1o'clock in the afternoon. My phone rang, it was one of my old friends, who needed help to find a person, who he could finance to go for Hajj. I told him that the passport and Hajj application of a person was waiting on my desk. He promised to send the money, but it was already too late as the bank was supposed to be closed in another fifteen minutes. A man in my office overheard the conversation and offered to help as he knew the bank manager. Before the end of the day, the application was submitted, money deposited and the man left for Hajj in time. It is a testament to the fact that this honour is only accorded by Allah ﷻ, one cannot earn it.

There was a man from Pakistan who spent his entire life in Masjid al-Haram. His only possession was a small bag and a stick. He was only seventeen when he went to Kaába and asked Allah ﷻ to allow him to stay in the Sacred House till his death. For fifty odd years, he stayed in *Baytullah*, disconnected from the rest of the world. He spent his days and nights just within the bounds of the Sacred House of Allah ﷻ. The man lived a life devoid of worldly desires, only to be close to his True Beloved. His only desire was to live and die near Kaába and Allah ﷻ fulfilled his desire. It is said that while reciting Qurán on a Friday afternoon, the Angel of death took his soul to meet his Beloved.

Stay humble, as Allah ﷻ has everything except for humility and this is a quality He adores in His slave. Beseech Him, seek everything you desire and He will fulfil. It is narrated from Imam Ghazali that Musa ﷺ, the Prophet of Allah asked Allah ﷻ the reason behind the great status awarded to the scholars of the Beloved Prophet Muhammad's ﷺ nation, as of the Prophets of Israelites. Allah ﷻ sent Imam Ghazali's soul to meet Musa's ﷺ soul. Musa ﷺ asked his name and Imam Ghazali started with his ancestry. Musa ﷺ said to him that he had only asked his name and there was no need to share the complete family history. Imam Ghazali replied, 'Musa ﷺ! Allah ﷻ asked you a simple question as to what you were holding in your hand and you told him that it was your stick and then you went on telling the uses of your stick.' Musa ﷺ replied, 'I was having the honour to talk to Allah ﷻ, so I wanted to prolong those moments.' Imam Ghazali replied, 'I cannot get that honour, but at least I can talk to you, who had that great honour to talk to Allah ﷻ.' Therefore, when you perform Hajj, cherish every moment, prolong your conversation with Allah ﷻ.

Arafat

It is a place where the slaves join their aspirations, devote their hearts to humble supplications and raise their hands to seek Allah's Mercy. On the day of Arafat, Shaytan can see Allah's mercy forgiving serious sins, the Beloved Prophet ﷺ said, *"Shaytan never appears smaller, more abject, more abased and more furious than on the day of Arafat."* [Malik]

This is the day which reminds one of the Day of Judgement, the crowd, loud voices begging for

Mercy in various languages just as the site of the Resurrection. Be certain that your supplications will be answered, so seek the blessings for every person of the Muslim Ummah. Remember the Beloved Prophet ﷺ said, *"Allah says, I am to my servant as he expects of Me. I am with him when he remembers Me. If he remembers Me in his heart, I remember him to Myself, and if he remembers me in an assembly, I mention him in an assembly better than his, and if he draws nearer to Me a hand's span, I draw nearer to him an arm's length, and if he draws nearer to Me an arm's length, I draw nearer to him a fathom's length, and if he comes to me walking, I rush to him at (great) speed."* [Bukhari and Muslim]

Try to find a place where you can focus and do not worry about others. Do not criticise anyone, just recall all the blessings of Allah ﷻ and show your appreciation. Seek His forgiveness for all the sins and supplicate for His Mercy and *Rahma* for the whole Ummah.

Ramy

Casting pebbles or Ramy is the Sunnah of Ibraheem ﷺ, since it was this place where Shaytan tried to dissuade him to follow the Command of Allah ﷻ and Ibraheem ﷺ pelted him with stones. You should be aware that even though, you cannot see Shaytan, but by acting to the Command of Allah ﷻ and following the Sunnah of the Prophet ﷺ, you are actually throwing stones in Shaytan's face. The only way to spite Shaytan is through the compliance with Command of Allah ﷻ in adherence to His Orders, without seeking reasons and justifications. Do not throw shoes or any other objects as the only way is the way of Sunnah. Again, beg Allah ﷻ that you are weak and the only way you can be saved from Shaytan's web is through Allah's ﷻ Mercy.

Sacrificing the Animal-Hady

Slaughtering of the sacrificial animal is a means to draw close to Allah ﷻ by virtue of obedience. Little of what is excellent is better than much that is inferior. Ibn Umar ؓ was going to sacrifice a Bactrian camel. He was offered a price of three hundred gold coins for it, so he asked the Beloved Prophet ﷺ, if he should sell it and use the money to buy several other camels, but the Beloved Prophet ﷺ told him, *'No, sacrifice it!'* [Abu Dáud]

He could have bought many animals for that money, but the objective is to purify the soul and adorn it with the beauty of reverence for Allah ﷻ. The devotion is shown by regard for excellence of quality in the value, not by quantity. As Allah ﷻ mentions in Qurán;

"Their flesh and blood do not reach Allah, yet your devotion reaches Him." [Qurán, al Hajj, 22:37]

Death upon Faith

Allah ﷻ commands the believers to die in complete submission to him, as mentioned in Qurán:

"O believers! Be mindful of Allah in the way He deserves, and do not die except in a state of full submission to Him."[Qurán, Aale Imran 3:102]

During every ritual of Hajj, supplicate Allah ﷻ to grant us death on faith. Say, *'La ilaha Illallah Mohammadur Rasoolullah'*, and beseech Allah ﷻ to grant us this testimony in the last breath, in the grave, on the Day of Resurrection, on the Bridge and the Scale. Make Allah ﷻ a witness to your testimony, in the Sacred House, Arafat, Mina and all the other Sacred Places.

VISITING MADINAH THE RADIANT

After Makkah, there is no place superior to Madinah, the city of the Messenger ﷺ. Deeds in the city of Madinah are compounded as the Beloved Prophet ﷺ said, *"One prayer in my Masjid is better than a thousand prayers in any other Masjid, except the Sacred Masjid (Baytullah)"* [Bukhari]

Every good deed in Madinah is rewarded thousand times more. Ibn Abbas ؓ narrated that the Beloved Prophet ﷺ said, *"One prayer in the Masjid of Madinah is worth ten thousand prayers, one prayer in the al-Aqsa is worth a thousand and one prayer in the Sacred House is worth a hundred thousand."* [Ibn Maja]

Madinah is a place of great reverence and demands extreme respect. You would notice that in Makkah, the believers would be calling upon Allah ﷻ, crying and screaming, begging for His *Rahma* and Mercy. However, Madinah the Radiant city of the Prophet ﷺ demands veneration in a very quiet manner. Allah ﷻ mentions in Qurán:

> *"Believers, do not raise your voices above the voice of the Prophet ﷺ and when speaking to him do not be loud as you are lound to one another, lest all your deeds are reduced to nothing without your even realising it."* [Qurán, al Hujarat 49:2]

This verse very clearly addresses the believers to be deferential and respectful in the city of the Beloved Prophet ﷺ. Rawdah, or "The Noble Garden", is an area between the minbar or pulpit and house of the Prophet ﷺ and Sayedda Ayesha ؓ. It is regarded as Riyaḍ al-Jannah, meaning 'Gardens of Paradise'. It is narrated by Abu Huraira ؓ, that the Beloved Prophet ﷺ said, *"Between my house and my pulpit there is a garden of the gardens of Paradise, and my pulpit is on my fountain tank (Al-Kauthar)."* [Bukhari 1196]

The scholars agree that the soil which is adjacent to the Rawdha or the Sacred chamber is more reverent to the Throne of Allah ﷻ as this touches the Beloved of Allah ﷺ. It is important that one understands the veneration of this city before even entering it, as any disrespectful act may erase all good deeds. Before entering Madinah, seek Allah's forgiveness. Cleanse your soul through repentance and ask Allah ﷻ to hide your sins from His Beloved ﷺ. When you enter the city, thank Allah ﷻ for according you the honour to visit the city of His Beloved Prophet ﷺ. As you enter Madinah, the Beloved Prophet ﷺ is your host and you are his guest. You are one out of billions who has been chosen for this special honour. You should acknowledge the fact and show your gratitude.

Everything which belongs to Madinah has an association to the Beloved Prophet ﷺ, therefore, do not criticise or find faults. It is narrated by Abu Huraira ؓ that the Beloved Prophet ﷺ said, *'If anyone endures the rigors and austerity (of Madinah), I shall be an intercessor for him on the Day of Judgement.'* [Muslim 1378]

It is narrated that a man while visiting Madinah bought some yoghurt. He did not like it and said that the yoghurt in Madinah was sour. That night, he was ordered by the Beloved Prophet ﷺ in his dream, to leave the city of Madinah. The man had disrespected Madinah and the Beloved Prophet ﷺ did not approve of it. He sought advice from a scholar and was advised to visit Sayeddina Hamza's ؓ grave and seek his intercession as the Beloved Prophet ﷺ loved him. He was advised by Sayedina Hamza ؓ in his dream, to leave the city and obey the orders of the Beloved Prophet ﷺ. Therefore, when you are in Madinah, take extreme caution in your actions and words.

Till the Day of Resurrection, the residents of Madinah are privileged to be the neighbours of the Beloved Prophet ﷺ, hence, they are honoured and privileged. None of us who is not a resident of Madinah can compare ourselves with any of them, therefore, take due care not to disrespect them.

Entering Madinah the Radiant

When your eyes alight on the city, remember this is the city Allah ﷻ selected for His Beloved Prophet ﷺ, a home selected for him from where he established his exemplary precedents and proclaimed Islam. Remember, Allah ﷻ cautioned against raising the voice above His Beloved Prophet's ﷺ voice. Show your gratitude to Allah ﷻ for granting you faith and according the permission to visit the city of His Beloved ﷺ. Behold the walls of the Masjid with love and yearning to be with him on the Day of Judgement.

This is the abode of the Prophet ﷺ. The soil which kissed the feet of the Beloved Prophet ﷺ is jubilant on the blessings awarded to it and envied by the stars of the sky. Imagine the streets of Madinah, which were honored to have the footprints of the Beloved Prophet ﷺ. Envision the time when the companions used to walk these grounds. Look at the Mount of Uhud with veneration as it had the honour of having the Beloved Prophet ﷺ on its top. This city and its surroundings are honoured as the Beloved Prophet's ﷺ blessed feet have trodden on this land, so walk these streets with dignity and caution.

Our elders illustrated great respect and veneration for the city of the Beloved Prophet ﷺ. Once, Imam Abu Hanifa رحمة الله عليه went to Madinah, just after three days, he asked his companions to depart from the city. The companions requested him to extend the stay for few more days. He agreed to stay for another day and then asked them to depart. When the companions asked for the reason, he told them that he had not consumed any food or water for last few days, in case he had to relieve himself in the blessed city of Madinah.

During his stay in Madinah, Imam Malik رحمۃ اللہ علیہ used to wear a new robe every day for the Hadith lesson and donated it the same day. When Mawlana Qasim Nanotawi رحمۃ اللہ علیہ went to visit Madinah, he took off his shoes before the city entrance and walked barefoot on the scorching hot path. Another man tried to follow him, but he could hardly place his feet on the ground. Mawlana Rasheed Ahmad Gangohi رحمۃ اللہ علیہ advised him to wear his shoes and said, 'Mawlana Qasim is in a state of veneration, where he cannot feel any pain.'

Visiting the Masjid

There are many sound and authentic narrations regarding the life of the Prophets after death, as Anas bin Malik رضی اللہ عنہ narrated that the Beloved Prophet ﷺ said, *"The Prophets are alive in their graves and are engaged in praying."* [Musnad Abi Yala:3425; Majma Az Zawaid, Zikar Al Ambiya, Vol:VIII pp, 276 Hadith:13812; Al-Albani, Silsilat al-aHadith al-Sahihah Vol:II, pp,187, Hadith:621]

Abdur Rahman Jami رحمۃ اللہ علیہ, the famous Persian poet had his heart filled with the ardent love of the Beloved Prophet ﷺ. It is narrated that he composed a beautiful ode in the praise of the

Beloved Prophet ﷺ and desired to read that in front of the Beloved Prophet's ﷺ *Rawdha*. As he was on his way to Madinah, in his dream, the Governor was told by the Beloved Prophet ﷺ to stop Jami ؓ from entering the city, however, Jami ؓ entered the city unnoticed. The Governor was cautioned to stop him and finally, the guards arrested him. The Beloved Prophet ﷺ told the Governor, in his dream that the man was not to be arrested. He was ordered to stop Jami ؓ because his poetry was filled with his ardent love for Beloved Prophet ﷺ and if he had read it in front of the Rawdha, the Beloved Prophet ﷺ would have met him. When the Governor told Jami ؓ, he promised to keep his emotions in control.

The path to Allah ﷻ is through following the Beloved Prophet ﷺ. Allah ﷻ has linked His Beloved Prophet's ﷺ remembrance with His own remembrance in the affirmation of faith: *"There is none worthy of worship but Allah ﷻ and Muhammad ﷺ is the Messenger of Allah."* There is no other way to Allah besides the way of the Beloved Prophet ﷺ. Once you reach Madinah, wash yourself, if possible, wear new clothes otherwise wear clean clothes before you go to Masjid. Get yourself ready as you do for a special occasion. On reaching the Masjid, recall that this is the place Allah ﷻ had chosen for His Beloved Prophet ﷺ and most virtuous of the Muslims. Enter this place with humility and veneration as this is the place where even angels seek permission. Keep your voice low in the city and especially when you are in the Masjid of the Beloved Prophet ﷺ. The Companions of the Beloved Prophet ﷺ kept their voices low even when they visited the Masjid after the Beloved Prophet ﷺ.

Visiting the Rawdah

There are many statements which have been written to prove the consensus by the great scholars which conform to the belief that the Prophets are alive in their graves. Hence, all the scholars of *Ahlus Sunnah Wal Jama'ah* have recorded *'Ijma'* consensus on this belief. The Beloved Prophet ﷺ said,

"Among the most excellent of your days is Friday; On this day Adam ﷺ was created; On this day shall be the Nafakhah(Trumpet); on it all creation will collapse. So, send a great dealing of blessing upon me on this day, for your blessings will be presented to me." The Companions asked, *'Allah's Messenger ﷺ! how can our blessing be submitted to*

you, when your body is decayed?' He ﷺ said, *'Allah has prohibited the earth from consuming the bodies of the Prophets.'"* [Sunan Ibn Maja Vol.1: Hadith:1626]

Allah's Messenger ﷺ said, *"Whoever visits my grave after my death, it is as he has visited me in my life."* [Tibrani Vol.012, Hadith:406; Bayhaqi Shab al-Iman Vol.III, Hadith:489]

The Beloved Prophet ﷺ said, *"If anyone of you greets me, Allah returns my soul to me and I respond to the greeting."* [Abu Dawud Book 004, Hadith Number 2036]

In the explanation of the Hadith, Imam Jalal ud-din Suyuti ﷺ wrote, "The word "*radda*" means `*ala al-dawam*," which means, permanently and not temporarily. In other words, Allah ﷻ does not return the *Ruh* and take it back, then return it again and then take it back, but He returned it to the Prophet ﷺ permanently and the Prophet ﷺ is alive permanently." [Al-Hawi lil Fatawi, Vol.2, p.271-272]

Before, presenting yourself, make some charity, perform two Rakás and send Salawat in abundance. Read Qaseeda Burda if you can which is an ode composed in the praise of the Beloved Prophet ﷺ. While you are in Riyad ul Jannah or Rawdha, please avoid using your phone to call someone or take photos. This place is not a tourist attraction, this is the Masjid and the abode of the Beloved Prophet ﷺ. While you are in such close proximity of the Beloved Prophet ﷺ and he is attentive towards you, it is extremely disrespectful to take photos. If someone else is taking photos, just ignore that person and stay focussed on your own objective.

It is commonly observed that when it is time for ladies, they run towards Riyad ul Jannah, screaming and pushing others. If anyone believes that by running and screaming in Riyad ul Jannah can bring her closer to the Beloved Prophet ﷺ, then it is a serious mistake. The place holds great reverence and demands extreme respect. By shoving and pushing other sisters in faith, one cannot win the Beloved Prophet's ﷺ approval. The same rules for respect apply to all believers whether men or women. You should only make your way towards *Rawdha* as far as you can go with due respect and without pushing others. If you cannot get too close to *Rawdha*, do not feel deprived or dejected. Stand somewhere quiet where you are not being pushed and send *Salawat* and benediction. The Beloved Prophet ﷺ can hear you and replies to your greetings.

When you approach the pulpit of the Beloved Prophet ﷺ, stand as if you would have stood before him. Approach as you would have approached his noble person. You are approaching the one who is most Beloved to Allah ﷻ and your intercessor before Allah ﷻ. Be extremely respectful and humble as he is aware of your presence, of your standing there and of your visit. He is receiving your greetings and benediction and replies to your greetings. Feel in your heart, the Beloved Prophet's ﷺ immense dignity and magnificence and keep sending Salawat or durood. Send benediction and greetings from your family, friends and even your enemies. Request the Beloved Prophet ﷺ to seek forgiveness for you, your family and the whole Ummah from Allah ﷻ. Allah ﷻ accepts the supplications of the Beloved Prophet ﷺ, so request him to beseech Allah ﷻ for all your needs.

As Riyad ul Jannah is a Garden of Paradise, beseech Allah ﷻ, requesting Him to enter you in Paradise as He has accorded this honour to you in this World. Supplicate to Allah ﷻ, "O Allah ﷻ! It was a tradition of the honourable to free slaves on the graves of the loved ones and You love when someone sets a slave free. Allah ﷻ! I am Your slave standing in front of your Beloved, in the Garden of Paradise, save me from Hellfire. Allah ﷻ! The

Prophet ﷺ is Your Beloved and Shaytan is Your enemy, if you free this slave from Hellfire, your Beloved will be pleased, Your enemy displeased and your slave will be saved. Allah ﷻ! I am in the Garden of Paradise, so grant me an abode in the eternal Garden as You promised that the Garden of Paradise is eternal and those who will enter, will stay there forever."

Thank Allah ﷻ for according you the honour to visit the city of His Prophet ﷺ and pray to Him to accord you this honour again. Seek forgiveness for any mistake or disrespectful action which may have occurred knowingly or unknowingly in the blessed city. Recite affirmation of faith (*Kalima*), and make Allah ﷻ and the Beloved Prophet ﷺ a witness to your testimony of faith;

لَا إِلٰهَ إِلَّا اللهُ مُحَمَّدٌ رَسُوْلُ اللهِ

"There is none worthy of worship but Allah ﷻ and Muhammad ﷺ is the Messenger of Allah."

Before departing from Madinah, visit Jannat al Baqée, the graveyard where family and the Companions of the Prophet ﷺ are buried.

Journey Homewards

At the end of this journey, the heart should be sad for one does not know whether the pilgrimage has been accepted or not. This can be ascertained by the conduct on the return from this journey. If you find your heart extremely adverse of the world and its delusion and inclined towards Allah ﷻ, then assume that the pilgrimage has been accepted. If you find following the commandments of Shariáh easy and your conduct in accordance with the Sacred Law, then Allah ﷻ has accepted your pilgrimage. When someone enquires about your journey, Praise Allah ﷻ and do not complain of any hardships related to the journey

Allah ﷻ accorded you the honour to visit the most Sacred cities on Earth, one which Allah ﷻ associates to Himself and the other to His Beloved Prophet ﷺ. If you still find the false glamour of this world appealing and your life does not change, then the journey was nothing but toil and hardship.

UMRAH

Umrah is the lesser pilgrimage, which can be performed any time during the year except the five days of Hajj from 9th of Dhul Hijjah to 13th Dhul Hijjah. Before the start of the journey, it is important to understand the boundaries of Haram which can be defined as a restricted zone where certain acts are deemed unlawful, which might be considered lawful in other areas. For example, it is prohibited to damage trees or plants, carry weapons, hunt animals, or graze animals and behave or fight in a manner that is sure to violate the decorum and sanctity of Masjid Al-Haram. However, in case of violation of any of the aforementioned laws, one must give Sadaqah or Damm as an expiation. Boundaries of Haram are as follows:

- ❖ Taneem which is located 3 miles or 5 kilometres from Makkah and at a distance of 5 miles or 8 kilometres from the Kaába. Also known as Masjid Taneem, Masjid Ayesha is located in the direction of Madinah at the boundary of Haram.

  - ❖ Adaat Laban is located on the route to Yemen which is 7 miles or 11 kilometres from Makkah.

- Wadi Nakhla is located on the route to Iraq, which is at a distance of 7 miles or 11 kilometres from Makkah.
- Arafat, is close to Masjid Al-Nimrah. It is located on the route to the city of Taif. The boundary of Arafat is 7 miles or 11 kilometres from Makkah.
- Ji'ranah is located about 9 miles or 14 kilometres from Makkah.
- Hudaibiyah also known as Masjid Al-Hudaibiyah is situated on the route to Jeddah, about 10 miles or 16 kilometres from Makkah.

Miqat

Literally meaning "a stated place or time," the Miqat line is where pilgrims intending to perform Umrah or Hajj must enter the state of Ihram before crossing the boundary.

- Dhul Hulayfah is the station of Miqat for those who live in Madinah and the surrounding areas. Every pilgrim coming for Hajj from the Northern direction should be dressed in Ihram before crossing Dhul Hulayfah. This place is also known as Abyar Ali, Dhul Hulayfah is eighteen kilometres southwest of

Masjid al-Nabwi in Madinah and 225 miles or 410 kilometres north of Makkah.

- ❖ Al-Juhfah is the Miqat for people travelling to perform Hajj from Sudan, Algeria, Egypt, Syria, Turkey, Europe, Northern America and other countries in Africa. Al-Juhfah is commonly known as Rabigh and it is situated 113 miles or 182 kilometres northwest of Makkah. It is named after the small town Rabigh, located at the north of Al-Juhfah. It is the place where the Beloved Prophet ﷺ met his uncle Abbas ؓ during his journey to conquest Makkah.

- ❖ Qarn al-Manazil is the Miqat for pilgrims travelling from Najd, UAE, Pakistan, Oman, Malaysia, Australia, Singapore, etc. It is located 50 miles or 80 kilometres east of Makkah, near the city of Taif and Riyadh. It is the same place where Jibrael ؑ appeared before the Beloved Prophet ﷺ when he was persecuted by the people of Taif.

- ❖ Dhat Irq is the Miqat for people who intend to perform Hajj from Russia, China, Iran and Iraq. It is situated 56 miles or 90 kilometres northeast of Makkah. Dhat Irq was established during the Caliphate of Umar ؓ soon after the conquest of Basra and Kufa. It is named after the largest mountain of the area, Irq Aswad.

- ❖ Yalamlam is the Miqat station for the pilgrims of Yemen and those travelling from the southern regions as Nigeria and South Africa. Also known as Al-Sadiah, Yalamlam is located 62 miles or 100 kilometres south of Makkah.
- ❖ Anyone living within the boundaries of Makkah can assume Ihram from where they start (the directional whereabouts of the station of Miqat). However, suppose a person decides to participate in Umrah or Hajj while being within the boundaries of Al-Haram (areas within the Sacred Sanctuary of Makkah). Al-Hil, to be exact, is the area between the boundaries of Haram and the boundaries of Miqat. The towns and cities, namely Khulais, Jeddah, Taneem and Al-Janun are situated within the Hil area. Therefore, pilgrims travelling through or residing within the Hil area must enter the state of Ihram before crossing the boundaries of Haram. Therefore, for the residents of Makkah, the stations of Miqat are as follows: Ji'ranah, the Mosque of Taneem and Hudaibiyah.

Wearing the Ihram

It is encouraged to get the hair cut (for men), trim nails and remove the unnecessary hair and perform ghusl before entering the state of Ihram. If ghusl is not possible, then perform wudu. After wudu or ghusl, men have to wear two unstitched sheets, one is wrapped around the waist and the other covers the upper body. It is encouraged to wear white sheets. Ladies wear their normal covered clothes. The Ihram for ladies is to cover their head fully, it is important to wear Niqab in a way, where cloth does not touch the face.

Then, perform two Raká with an intention of repentance or Tawba, seek forgiveness for all the sins and send Salawat or blessings upon the Beloved Prophet ﷺ. It is Sunnah to perform two Raká salat before making the intention of Ihram. After Surah Fatiha, recite Surah al Kafiroon in the first Raká and Surah Ikhlaas in the second, otherwise any other Surahs can also be recited. If a woman is menstruating at the time of entering the state of Ihram, she does not need to perform the two Raká Salah and just make the intention.

After the two Raká, men should remove the head covering or cap and make the intention for Hajj or Umrah accordingly.

The intention for Umrah would be,

"O Allah ﷻ! I intend to perform Umrah, make it easy for me and accept it."

For Hajj Qiran the intention would be,

"O Allah ﷻ! I intend to perform Umrah and Hajj together, make it easy for me and accept it."

For Hajj Ifraad, the intention would be,

"O Allah ﷻ! I intend to perform Hajj, make it easy for me and accept it."

For Hajj Tamattu, the intention for Hajj would be made once the Umrah is done and before the rituals of Hajj start. Therefore, the first intention would be,

"O Allah ﷻ! I intend to perform Umrah, make it easy for me and accept it."

It is must to recite Talbiyah once, reciting three times is Sunnah. Men should recite Talbiyah in a loud voice whereas women should recite in a low voice. Talbiyah is to be recited by the tongue, saying it in heart does not suffice the condition. Ihram is completed only by making the intention or niyah and reciting Talbiyah.

لَبَّيْكَ اللَّهُمَّ لَبَّيْكَ، لَبَّيْكَ لاَ شَرِيكَ لَكَ لَبَّيْكَ، إِنَّ الْحَمْدَ وَالنِّعْمَةَ لَكَ وَالْمُلْكَ لاَ شَرِيكَ لَكَ

Labbayka Allāhumma labbayk. Labbayk lā shareeka laka labbayk. Inna al-ḥamda, wa n-'imata, Laka wal mulk. Lā shareeka lak.

"Here I am, O Allah, here I am, here I am. You have no partner, here I am. Verily all praise and blessings are Yours, and all sovereignty. You have no partner."

The pilgrim must continue reciting Talbiyah throughout the journey. Once Talbiyah is recited, all the conditions of Ihram are applicable. Once the pilgrim enters the state of Ihram, a pilgrim cannot cut nails or hair, apply perfume or have sexual intercourse. Men are not allowed to cover their head or face or wear stitched clothes. Women wear their stitched clothes however, the head or face covering shall not touch the face. The pilgrim who had the intention of Hajj Tamattu will stop reciting Talbiyah after reaching Makkah, before performing Tawaf.

For pilgrims with an intention of Hajj Ifraad and Hajj Qiran, Talbiyah will be recited till *Rami* is performed on the tenth of Dhul Hijjah.

Rules for Entering Miqat

- If the pilgrim is coming by air, he/she must enter the state of Ihram before the aeroplane enters the boundary of Miqat.
- Any adult, sane Muslim entering the boundaries of Miqat, whether by air or land and intends to enter Haram must enter the state of Ihram before Miqat, even if the purpose of travel is business or recreation.
- Anyone who does not enter the state of Ihram and violates the condition is liable to *Damm* or expiation.
- Each and every time a person violates the boundaries of Miqat, he/she is liable to expiation or Damm.
- If the person returns to Miqat and makes the intention for Umrah or Hajj and enters the state of Ihram, then the expiation is invalidated.
- If a person is flying to Jeddah and has no intention of performing Umrah or Hajj or visiting Haram, then he/she does not have to enter the state of Ihram.
- Those residing between Miqat and Haram can enter Haram or Makkah without entering the state of Ihram only if they have no intention of performing Umrah or Hajj. If they have an

intention of performing Umrah or Hajj, they must wear Ihram.

Circumambulation-Tawaf

Tawaf is one of the principal rites of the pilgrimage and refers to walking in circles around the Kaába in an anti-clockwise motion. One Tawaf comprises of seven complete circuits, with each one starting and ending at Hajr e Aswad the Black Stone.

To prepare for the Tawaf, the pilgrim must ensure wudu or ablutions have been performed. Men should pass the upper garment of the Ihram sheet under the right arm and over the left shoulder, thus leaving the right shoulder bare which is called 'iddtibaa'. When you reach the Black Stone (al-Hajar al-Aswad), you have arrived at the starting point for the Tawaf, and you may cease reciting the Talbiyah. The intention for Umrah is to be made as:

"O Allah, I perform Tawaf of Umrah to please You. Make it easy for me and accept it from me."

Istilam

If space permits, move right, stand before the Black Stone and kiss it. If you are unable to move close enough to kiss the Black Stone, you may touch it by hand. If you are unable to kiss or touch the Black Stone, raise your hands, palms facing outwards, and say:

بِسْمِ اللهِ وَاللهُ أَكْبَرُ

This alternative is perfectly acceptable so there is no need for pushing or shoving which may harm yourself or others if you are not able to reach the Black Stone. This act, whether you kiss the Black Stone, touch it by hand or utter a prayer while pointing by the palm of your hands towards the Black Stone is called *Istilam*. You may now begin your seven circumambulations, moving to the right so that you keep the Kaába to your left, counter-clockwise, around the Kaába.

While performing Tawaf, there are no prescribed prayers but there are a number of supplications which are recommended. You may also use the prayers that form part of your daily prayer sessions and pray to Allah ﷻ in your own way in your own language.

Hateem is a semi-circular section which originally formed part of the Kaába but was not incorporated into the Kaába when the Kaába was rebuilt. When you reach the fourth corner of the Kaába called

Rukn Yemani, touch it with your right hand or both hands and, as you walk between Rukn Yemani and the Black Stone, you may pray:

اَللّٰهُمَّ اِنِّی اَسْئَلُكَ الْعَفْوَ وَالْعَافِيَةَ فِی الدُّنْيَا وَالْاٰخِرَةِ رَبَّنَا اٰتِنَا فِی الدُّنْيَا حَسَنَةً وَّفِی الْاٰخِرَةِ حَسَنَةً وَّقِنَا عَذَابَ النَّارِ

(O Allah! I seek mercy and to be save from affliction in this world and hereafter)

When you reach the Black Stone, perform Istilam again, to mark the start of your second circumambulation. Continue in the same way, until you have completed the seven circumambulations, including Istilam at the end of each circuit.

Between the Black Stone and the door of the Kaába is the sacred place, which is called *Multazam*. If you are able to reach this place, supplicate Allah ﷻ for His mercy and for His beneficence. If you are prevented by the number of people from reaching Multazam, simply face towards the area and make your prayers. On completion of the seven circumambulations, approach Maqam e Ibrahim (the Station of Ibrahim ﷺ) and offer two Rakaá, drink Zamzam and pray to Allah ﷻ.

Ramal

When performing the first three circumambulations, men uncover their right arm and move with quick, short steps, sticking the chest out which is called *Ramal*. The remaining four circumambulations should be performed at a normal walking pace.

Sáe

After Tawaf, move towards Safa, you are to perform Sa'e, the laps or circuit between the two hills of Safa and Marwah. As you approach Safa, recite the Quranic verse:

"Verily, Safa and Marwah are among the shrines of Allah".

Face the Kaába and make intention,

"O Allah ﷻ! I make the intention of performing Saé between the Safa and the Marwah to achieve Your pleasure (rida). Make it easy for me and accept it."

Do not raise your hands when you make the intention. Intention can be made through tongue or in heart, it does not have to be in Arabic, you can make the intention in your own language. After you have made the intention then raise hands as in supplication and say Allahu Akbar three times, then recite the fourth Kalima, as follows:

$$\text{لَا إِلٰهَ إِلَّا اللّٰهُ وَحْدَهُ لَا شَرِيْكَ لَهُ لَهُ الْمُلْكُ وَلَهُ الْحَمْدُ يُحْيِىْ وَيُمِيْتُ بِيَدِهِ الْخَيْرُ وَهُوَ عَلٰى كُلِّ شَىْءٍ قَدِيْرٌ}$$

(There is none worthy of worship besides Allah, He has no partners, for Him is the kingdom and all praise, He is the giver of life and death, in His decree is all good and His power rules over everything)

Then, send durood or Salawat to the Beloved Prophet ﷺ and make supplication as this is a place where supplications are accepted. Then, proceed towards Marwah, walking at a normal pace. Men do not need to uncover their shoulders. For men, once they reach the green marker, if they are able, they should run until they reach the next green marker, whereupon they should revert to a normal walking pace. Women should proceed at normal walking pace throughout. The area between the two markers is where Hajira ؑ heard her baby Ismael ؑ crying and she ran looking for help. The Beloved Prophet ﷺ made the following supplication between the specified area:

رَبِّ اغْفِرْ وَارْحَمْ إِنَّكَ أَنْتَ الْأَعَزُّ الْأَكْرَمُ

(O Lord! Forgive and have mercy, indeed You are the Venerable, the Generous)

When you stand on Marwah, face the Qiblah, and repeat the prayers and supplications as you did at Safa. This is one circuit of Saé completed. Repeat the same procedure until you have completed seven circuits, ending your Saé at Marwah. While performing Saé, you should beseech Allah ﷻ and supplicate.

Shaving and Trimming Hair-Halq and Taqsir

Halq refers to the act of shaving the entire head and Taqsir means trimming the hair on the head by at least an inch. Performing Halq or Taqsir is the Wajib (obligatory) act that must be performed in order to leave the state of Ihram. On completion of Saé, if possible then perform two Rakáa Salat in the Haram. Then, men must shave their heads or cut their hair. Women should clip their hair one or two centimetres. Women can cut their own hair, but they should not drop their hair in the Masjid nor should they get the hair cut from anyone other than their Mahram or another woman. The Umrah rituals are now concluded and the pilgrim may change into every day clothes. The prohibitions on conduct during Umrah are now ended.

HAJJ

Hajj is performed on specific dates each year. Within the Islamic calendar, Hajj is performed between 8th to 12th of Dhul Hijjah – the last month of the Islamic year. For Hajj to be obligatory, one has to be an adult Muslim, free and sane.

- ❖ One has to be physically and mentally fit to perform the rituals of Hajj.
- ❖ One has to have sufficient funds to provide for the family till the pilgrim returns to the family.
- ❖ One has to have enough funds for undertaking the journey.
- ❖ The route for the journey be safe.
- ❖ For a woman, it is obligatory that she should be accompanied by a Mahram.

There are three forms of Hajj: *Tamattu, Ifraad and Qiran.*

- ❖ **Hajj Ifraad**: This is the form of Hajj when the pilgrim wears the Ihram only for Hajj.
- ❖ **Hajj Tamattu**: This is the form of Hajj when the pilgrim makes the intention to perform

Umrah and Hajj both. The pilgrim first enters the state of Ihram with the intention of Umrah. After Umrah is performed the pilgrim does not return home and then enters the state of Ihram for Hajj. Such pilgrim is called *Mutamattu*.

- **Hajj Qiran:** This is the form of Hajj when the pilgrim performs Hajj without getting out of the state of Ihram after performing Umrah

Obligatory Actions-Fard

- Ihram
- Staying in Arafat
- Farewell Tawaf

Obligations-Wajib

- On the tenth of Dhul Hijjah, leave Muzdhalfa after the sunrise
- Saé between Safa and Marwah
- Rami at Jamarat, which is throwing pebbles
- Getting the hair shaved or cut in the Haram during the prescribed days
- Farewell Tawaf before returning home
- Sacrificing animal for a pilgrim who is performing Hajj Tamattu or Qiran

- ❖ Performing Rami, sacrifice and shaving/cutting the hair in proper sequence
- ❖ Performing Tawaf called as Tawaf e Ziarat on either tenth, eleventh or twelfth of Dhul Hijjah

Sunnah

- ❖ Tawaf al Qudoom which is the arrival Tawaf is Sunnah for the pilgrims who are performing Hajj Ifraad or Hajj Qiran
- ❖ Ramal which is the brisk walk with chest sticking out during the first three circuits of Tawaf
- ❖ 'Iddtibaa' which is only for men, where the upper garment of the Ihram sheet is taken under the right arm and over the left shoulder, thus leaving the right shoulder bare
- ❖ Staying in Mina from eighth of Dhul Hijjah
- ❖ On the Day of Arafah, departure from Mina after the sunrise
- ❖ Spending the night of Yum al Nahr in Muzdalfah
- ❖ Taking a bath in Arafat

Eighth Dhul Hijjah

The first day of Hajj is known as Yawm al-Tarwiyah (the Day of Quenching Thirst). It was given this name because on this day, the early pilgrims were instructed to drink a lot of water and fill their containers in preparation for the long journey ahead. They would also make sure their animals were properly fed and had consumed enough water to allow them to travel to their destination. On this day the pilgrim has to leave Makkah for Mina after sunrise. The pilgrim should perform Dhur, Asar, Maghrib and Isha Salah in Mina.

Ninth Dhul Hijjah

- ❖ Perform the Fajr Salah in Mina.
- ❖ Leave for Arafat after sunrise.
- ❖ Perform Dhur and Asar Salah at the prescribed time. If the pilgrim performs the Salah in Masjid al Nimrah, then the two prayers are performed together.
- ❖ Make dua and continue beseeching Allah ﷻ. On this day a sermon is delivered from Masjid al-Nimra on Mount Arafah. Remember to listen to the khutbah if possible. The day of Arafah is one of the most important days for

Muslims, as Allah ﷻ, in Surah al-Maidah of the Holy Qurán, refers to the Day of Arafah as the Day on which He perfected His religion, completed His favours upon His Beloved Prophet Muhammad ﷺ, and approved Islam as a way of life.

❖ Leave for Muzdalfah after the sunset. Do not perform Maghrib Salah in Arafat or on the way to Muzdalfah. Muzdalfah is an open valley located at the southeast of Mina, on the way between Mount Arafat and Mina. Upon reaching there at sunset, the pilgrims pray the combined Salah of Maghrib and Isha and spend the night under the open sky.

❖ Ishaá and Maghrib Salah is performed together upon reaching Muzdalfah. First perform the Fard for Maghrib, then Fard for Ishaá. Then perform Sunnah for Maghrib and Ishaá, followed by Witr.

❖ Pick seventy pebbles for Rami.

❖ The pilgrim has to spend the night in Muzdalfah

Tenth Dhul Hijjah

After performing Fajr Salah you will depart Muzdalfah to go towards Mina. Remember to continuously recite the Talbiyah. The 10th of Dhul

Hijjah is called the Yawm al-Nahr, or the Day of Sacrifice. For pilgrims of Hajj, this is the day of pelting pebbles at one of the Jamarat, as well as sacrificing an animal. For the rest of the Muslims around the world, this is the day of Eid. The pilgrim has to be in Muzdalfah in the morning of tenth Dhul Hijjah from dawn to before sunrise and Fajr Salah is to be performed in Muzdalfah. Before sunrise, the pilgrim needs to leave for Mina and perform the first Rami.

The Rami (Stoning of the Devil)

Stoning of the Jamarat – sometimes referred to as the "Stoning of the Devil" – is a ritual carried out by Hajj pilgrims whereby pebbles are thrown at three stone structures in Mina. The act of throwing stones at the Jamarat is known as "Rami". The ritual of Rami is symbolic of the actions of Ibrahim ﷺ when he was faced with the trial of having to sacrifice his son, Ismail ﷺ.

On the way to carry out the commandment, Shaytan repeatedly tried to dissuade Ibrahim's ﷺ. As Ibrahim reached Jamarat al-Aqaba, he was instructed by Angel Gibrael ﷺ to throw seven stones at Shaytan and Shaytan fled. The three Jamarat indicate the three places where Shaytan tried to dissuade Ibrahim ﷺ from obeying the command of Allah ﷻ.

Once you reach Jamarat, you will head to Jamarat al-Aqaba, which is the big pillar, and here you will throw the first seven pebbles at the concrete pillar. As you throw the pebbles, you'll say the *takbir* اللهُ أَكْبَر (Allāhu 'Akbar): "Allah is The Greatest" upon each throw.

Following the sacrifice, you will proceed to Halq or Taqsir meaning shave or trim your hair if you are male. The Beloved Prophet Muhammad ﷺ shaved his hair and this is preferable. A woman trims her hair by the length of a fingertip.

Now you are allowed to leave the state of Ihram and wear comfortable clothing. You are also allowed to do things like wearing perfume etc. that was unlawful during your state of Ihram, except engaging in sexual intimacy. It is Sunnah to apply perfume as the Prophet Muhammad ﷺ smelt strongly of musk at this point.

You will now go to Makkah to perform *Tawaf al-ifadha* and Saé as part of your Hajj rituals. Tawaf al-ifada and Sáe are obligatory. You must perform them after the Rami, sacrifice and shaving (or trimming) of the head. On 10th and 12th Dhul Hijjah, the Tawaf and Sáe can be done.

- ❖ The time of the first Rami is from the sunrise of 10th to 11th Dhul Hijjah. It is Sunnah to perform Rami between sunrise and midday. It is permissible to perform Rami between midday to sunset, however after sunset it is Makrooh meaning disliked or not recommended. Performing Rami between dawn and sunrise on the tenth of Dhul Hijjah is also Makrooh or not recommended.
- ❖ The pilgrim would stop reciting Talbiyah before Rami.
- ❖ Pilgrims performing Hajj Tamattu and Qiran must sacrifice the sacrificial animal after Rami. Sacrifice is not obligatory for the pilgrim who has made the intention of Hajj Ifraad.
- ❖ Men have to shave or cut their hair. Women have to trim their hair by about half an inch. Ladies can trim their hair themselves or from another woman or their Mahram.
- ❖ After the hair is shaved or trimmed, Ihram is finished and men can wear normal stitched clothes. For the pilgrim performing Hajj Ifraad, it is optional to sacrifice an animal but trimming the hair is obligatory.

- **Tawaf Ziarat** is obligatory and needs to be performed after the sunrise of 10th Dhul Hijjah to before the sunset on 12th of Dhul Hijjah. If the pilgrim performs Tawaf Ziarat after the sunset of twelfth of Dhul Hijjah, then Damm or penalty occurs.

Eleventh Dhul Hijjah

Days 4 and 5 which is 11th and 12th Dhul Hijjah are known as "Ayyam al-tashreeq", or the days of drying meat. During the time of the Prophet ﷺ, pilgrims would preserve the Qurbani meat by seasoning and drying them under the sun. You are required to stay in Mina and complete two more Rami rituals on 11th and 12th Dhul Hijjah. On the afternoon of 11th Dhul Hijjah, you'll have your 21 pebbles ready and proceed to stone the three Jamarah.

You will begin with Jamarah al-Ula (the small pillar), then Jamarah al-Wusta (the middle pillar) and finally, Jamarah al-Aqaba (the big pillar). Each one should be stoned with seven consecutive pebbles accompanied by *takbeer*. You will stop after the first and middle Jamrah to make du'a facing the Qibla. Remember to take your spare pebbles with you in case you lose some. Once this is completed, you will return to your camp in Mina and spend the rest of the day in worship, making the most of the remaining time you have.

You will then repeat the same for the following day and stone the three Jamrah. It is recommended or Mustahab to perform Rami by sunset and after sunset till dawn, it is Makruh or detestable.

Twelfth Dhul Hijjah

Perform Rami at the three Jamrah, it is recommended or Mustahab to perform Rami by sunset. From after sunset till dawn, it is Makruh or detestable. Please note if you stay in Mina till the dawn of thirteenth, then it is obligatory to perform Rami on thirteenth as well.

Farewell Tawaf

After Tawaf Ziarat, Farewell Tawaf has to be performed before leaving Makkah. Ibn Abbas ؓ narrated: *"The people were ordered to perform the Tawaf al-wida as the last thing before leaving (Makkah), except the menstruating women who were excused."* [Bukhari]

If one performed Tawaf after Tawaf Ziarat but forgot to make an intention for the farewell Tawaf, it will still be considered as Farewell Tawaf.

TRANSGRESSIONS AND PENALTIES

Fidyah or penalty is obligatory if the pilgrim violates:

- Prohibitions of Ihram, such as applying perfume or cutting the hair.
- Failed to perform an obligatory or Wajib act of Hajj for example, missing the Rami or pelting of the Jamarat, or did not enter into Ihram from the Miqat etc.
- Transgressed the sanctity of the Haram such as hunting an animal or cutting a tree within its boundaries.

There are three categories of penalty, depending on the nature of the transgression:

Badanah

Offering a large sacrificial animal such as a camel or a cow (the size of which normally constitutes seven parts).

Damm

Offering a small sacrificial animal such as a sheep or a goat (or the cost of one-seventh of a large animal if sharing).

Sadaqah

Offering charity to the poor, normally in the form of food such as flour, wheat, barley, dates or raisins. Depending on the violation, the amount of Sadaqah falls into three categories:

- **Complete Sadaqah al-Fitr** – This is equivalent to about 3 kg of wheat, 6 kg of barley or 6 kg of dates or raisins or its value in money.
- **Less than Sadaqah al-Fitr** – This can be a handful of wheat or an equivalent.
- **Sadaqah equivalent to the value** – For example, cutting trees or grass in the boundaries of the Haram will necessitate Sadaqah equivalent to the value of those mistakes. The amount due will be judged by two Muslim men who are local to the area and upright in their character.

VIOLATION OF IHRAM

Entering Miqat

Entering the Miqat without coming into state of Ihram. The penalty will be waived by returning to the Miqat and re-entering into Ihram.	Damm

Fragrance

To apply perfume or something with fragrance e.g. fragranced tissue on any large areas of the body even for a moment, without a valid reason. Please note, large areas of the body refers to body parts such as the head, ankle, beard, hand, palm, thigh, calf, etc.	Damm
To apply perfume or something with fragrance e.g. fragranced tissue on any small areas of the body even for a moment, without a valid reason. Please note, small areas of the body refers to body parts such as the nose, finger, ear etc	Sadaqah al Fitr
To apply a large quantity of fragranced substances to any part of the body.	Damm
To apply small quantities of fragranced substances to various parts of the body so the total area of the body covered is equivalent to that of a large part of the body.	Damm
If the total area is not equivalent to that of a large body part.	Sadaqah al-Fitr
To use fragranced substances at different places. Damm will be incurred at each place.	Damm
There is no penalty if perfume is applied after wearing the Ihram garments and before making the	

intention for Ihram, even though the fragrance may remain thereafter. If the fragrance is washed off immediately after applying it, the penalty is still due. The fragrance should be washed off immediately touching it or leaving the fragrance on your body can result in further penalties.	
To apply a large amount of fragrance to a small area of clothing (less than one hand span) and wear the clothing for 12 hours or more. If a small amount of fragrance is applied to a large area of clothing (more than one hand span), the penalty is the same.	Damm
To apply a large amount of fragrance to a large area of clothing and wear the clothing for less than 12 hours. If a small amount of fragrance is applied to a small area of clothing, the penalty is the same.	Sadaqah al-Fitr
To wear clothes that have been dyed in saffron or safflower for 12 hours or more.	Damm
If the dyed clothing has been worn for less than 12 hours	Sadaqah al-Fitr
To wear clothes that have been incensed a lot for 12 hours or more.	Damm
If the incensed clothing has been worn for less than 12 hours or it is not incensed much.	Sadaqah al-Fitr

To touch al-Hajar al-Aswad, al-Rukn al-Yamani or the Multazam to the extent that a lot of fragrance becomes attached to the face or hands. Istilam can be done by gesturing to al-Hajar al-Aswad from far with your hands and kissing them.	Damm
If the aforementioned parts of the Kaaba are touched and a small amount of fragrance becomes attached to the hands or face.	Sadaqah al-Fitr
If the predominant ingredient in a product is a fragrance and it is used once, e.g. using fragrant soap to wash your hands. If the predominant ingredient in a product is not a fragrance, Sadaqah al-Fitr is due. However, if it is used more than once, Damm is required.	Damm

Wearing Stitched Clothing (For Men)

To wear clothing that is stitched or tailored to fit the shape of the body for 12 hours or more.	Damm
To wear the clothing for less than 12 hours, is due. If it is worn for less than an hour, a handful of wheat can be given as Sadaqah.	Sadaqah al-Fitr
If a person wears a stitched garment that has also been perfumed, two Damms are due upon him; one for	Two Damms

wearing the stitched garment and one for using a fragrance.

- ❖ If the pilgrim, in the state of Ihram, wears the stitched clothing for a number of consecutive days, a second Damm is necessary after one or two days.
- ❖ If a number of stitched garments are worn for a period of time such as shirt, trousers and underwear, the penalty will still be a single Damm.
- ❖ If an item of stitched clothing is worn in a manner in which it is not normally worn, for example, wearing a cloak as a loin cloth, no penalty is due. A penalty is only due when stitched garments are worn in the manner in which they are normally worn.
- ❖ It is permissible to cover yourself with a stitched blanket or duvet or any other type of covering, provided that it doesn't cover the face or the head.
- ❖ It is permissible to wrap the lower part of the body with a blanket, duvet or another type of covering.
- ❖ It is permissible to wear another layer of Ihram, on top of the Ihram that is currently being worn.
- ❖ It is permissible to wear a money belt / waist pouch / string which helps to further secure the lower garment of the Ihram.

Footwear

For a man to wear prohibited footwear for 12 hours or more.	Damm
If the footwear is worn for less than 12 hours.	Sadaqah al-Fitr

Covering the Head / Face

For a man to cover at least a quarter of the face or head for 12 hours or more.	Damm
If less than a quarter of the face / head is covered for 12 hours or more.	Sadaqah al-Fitr
If less than a quarter of the face / head is covered for 12 hours or more.	Sadaqah al-Fitr
For a woman to cover the whole face for 12 hours or more.	Damm
If the face / head is covered for less than 12 hours.	Sadaqah al-Fitr
For a person who is in the state of Ihram to cover the face or head of another person who is asleep, in the state of Ihram.	Damm
For the head or face to become covered accidentally while sleeping.	Sadaqah al-Fitr

Shaving, Cutting & Removing Hair

To remove a quarter or more of the hair on the head (or beard), voluntarily or otherwise.	Damm
If less than a quarter of the hair is shaved on the head (or beard), voluntarily or otherwise.	Sadaqah al-Fitr

To remove hair from one or both of the armpits or below the navel.	Damm
To remove the hair from the chest, thigh, ankle, shoulder or the upper and lower lip.	Sadaqah al-Fitr
Three or less strands of hair fall out while scratching or touching the head or are removed.	For each strand, a handful of wheat as Sadaqah.
If more than three hair fall out while scratching or touching the head or are removed.	Sadaqah al-Fitr
Halq or Taqsir outside the boundary of the Haram.	Damm
To remove a quarter of the hair before its due time e.g. before Sáe of Umrah or before the Hady of Hajj.	Damm
To cut the hair before Rami on the 10th of Dhul Hijjah or cut hair after Rami but before sacrifice.	Damm
To delay cutting the hair after sunset on 12th Dhul Hijjah.	Damm

Clipping the Nails

To clip all the nails of both hands and feet in one sitting. The same penalty is due if the nails are clipped from only one hand and one foot in one sitting.	Damm

| To clip less than five nails in one sitting or separate sittings. | Sadaqah al-Fitr for each nail |

Sexual Relations

- ❖ If Hajj or Umrah is nullified, all the rites will still have to be completed as normal while abstaining from all the other prohibitions of Ihram.
- ❖ A person whose Hajj or Umrah has been nullified cannot leave the state of Ihram until all the rites have been completed.
- ❖ If Hajj or Umrah is nullified, it will have to be repeated again or as soon as possible (even if it was a Nafl Hajj or Umrah).
- ❖ If sexual relations take place at different times and different places, a penalty is due for each occasion.
- ❖ Having a wet dream does not incur a penalty, although it does necessitate Ghusl (shower) and the clothing to be cleaned properly.
- ❖ For a Mufrid (someone performing Hajj al-Ifrad), only Hajj has to be repeated and not the Umrah.

| To enter Ihram for Umrah or Hajj in a state of Janabat (major ritual impurity requiring a bath). | Hajj and Umrah nullified and must be repeated. |

To have sexual relations, whether intentionally or forgetfully, after coming into Ihram for Hajj and before Wuquf in Arafat.	Damm Hajj nullified and must be repeated.
For a Qarin (someone performing Hajj al-Qiran – combined Hajj and Umrah) to have sexual relations after Tawaf al-Umrah and Wuquf in Arafat, but before Halq / Taqsir and Tawaf al-Ziyarah.	One Badanah and one Damm Hajj and Umrah still valid.
For a Qarin to have sexual relations after Tawaf al-Umrah but before Wuquf in Arafat.	Two Damms. Hajj nullified and must be repeated, Umrah still valid.
For a Qarin to have sexual relations before Tawaf al-Umrah and Wuquf in Arafat.	Two Damms Hajj and Umrah nullified and must be repeated.
To kiss, touch or embrace a person of the opposite gender with lust / desire.	Damm Hajj still valid
To have sexual relations at any point between Wuquf in Arafat and before Tawaf al-Ziyarah.	Badanah Hajj still valid
To have sexual relations after cutting the hair but before Tawaf al-Ziyarah.	Badanah Hajj still valid

To have sexual relations before starting Tawaf al-Umrah.	Damm Hajj still valid
To have sexual relations after completing the Tawaf and Sáe of Umrah but before cutting the hair.	Damm Umrah nullified and must be repeated
	Damm Umrah still valid

VIOLATION OF THE RITES

To perform even one circuit in a state of major ritual impurity (requiring Ghusl), in a state of menstruation or without Wudhu.	Damm	Penalty is waived if Tawaf is repeated
To complete the Umrah and thereafter coming into Ihram for another Umrah without cutting or shaving the hair.	Damm	Second Umrah must be completed before cutting the hair.
Cutting the hair before the second Umrah is completed	Two Damms.	

| would necessitate two Damms. | | |

Tawaf al-Qudum

- This Tawaf is Sunnah for an Afaqi (person who lives outside the Miqat boundaries) performing Hajj al-Qiran or Hajj al-Ifrad.
- Those performing Hajj al-Tamattu and Umrah, including the Afaqi, are exempt from performing this Tawaf.
- Those who reside within the boundaries of the Haram are also exempt from performing this Tawaf. It is only Mustahabb (recommended) for the resident of Makkah upon leaving the Miqat and re-entering to perform Hajj al-Qiran or Hajj al-Ifrad.

To perform this Tawaf without Wudhu. Penalty is waived if Tawaf is repeated.	Sadaqah al-Fitr for each circuit
To omit one, two or three circuits without a valid reason. Penalty is waived if Tawaf is repeated.	Sadaqah al-Fitr for each circuit
To omit four or more circuits without a valid reason. Penalty is waived if Tawaf is repeated.	Damm

To perform the Tawaf in a state of major ritual impurity (requiring Ghusl), in a state of menstruation or after child birth. Penalty is waived if Tawaf is repeated.	Damm

Tawaf al-Nafl

To perform less than four circuits without Wudu. Penalty is waived if Tawaf is repeated with wudu	Sadaqah al-Fitr for each circuit
To perform the entire Tawaf, or more than four circuits without Wudu. Penalty is waived if Tawaf is repeated with wudu	Damm
To omit one, two or three circuits without a valid reason. The penalty will be waived if the Tawaf is repeated.	Sadaqah al-Fitr for each circuit
To omit four or more circuits without a valid reason. The penalty will be waived if the Tawaf is repeated.	Damm

Tawaf al-Ziyarah

To delay Tawaf al-Ziyarah until after sunset on the 12th of Dhul Hijjah without a valid reason.	Damm
To perform less than four circuits without Wudhu. The penalty will be waived if the Tawaf is repeated.	Sadaqah al-Fitr for each circuit

To perform the entire Tawaf or more than four circuits without Wudhu. The penalty will be waived if the Tawaf is repeated.	Damm
To perform the Tawaf in a state of major ritual impurity (requiring Ghusl), in a state of menstruation or after child birth. The penalty will be waived if the Tawaf is repeated and performed in a state of ritual purity, even after 12th of Dhul Hijjah.	Badanah
To have sexual relations (including kissing and touching with desire) after cutting the hair but before Tawaf al-Ziyarah.	Damm Hajj is still valid

Tawaf al-Umrah

To perform even one circuit in a state of major ritual impurity (requiring Ghusl), in a state of menstruation or without Wudhu. The penalty will be waived if the Tawaf is repeated.	Damm
To omit this Tawaf completely.	Damm
To complete the Umrah and thereafter coming into Ihram for another Umrah without cutting or shaving the hair. The second Umrah must be completed before cutting the hair.	Damm
Cutting the hair before the second Umrah is completed would necessitate two Damms.	Two Damms.

Tawaf al-Wida

To omit the Tawaf entirely. The penalty will be waived by returning to the Miqat, re-entering into Ihram and performing Tawaf.	Damm
To perform this Tawaf without Wudhu. Penalty will be waived if Tawaf is repeated.	Sadaqah al-Fitr for each circuit
To omit one, two or three circuits without a valid reason. Penalty will be waived if Tawaf is repeated.	Sadaqah al-Fitr for each circuit
To omit four or more circuits without a valid reason. Penalty will be waived if Tawaf is repeated.	Damm
To perform the Tawaf in a state of major ritual impurity (requiring Ghusl), in a state of menstruation or after child birth. Women in this state are excused from the Tawaf if their departure cannot be delayed.	Damm

Sáe of Hajj and Umrah

Sáe performed without Wudhu is valid and won't incur a penalty. No penalty is due if there are breaks in between circuits.

To omit all seven circuits without a valid reason. The penalty will be waived if the Sáe is repeated.	Damm

To omit four or more circuits without a valid reason. The penalty will be waived if the Sáe is repeated.	Damm
Less than four circuits are omitted.	Sadaqah al-Fitr for each circuit

Mina

For those performing Hajj al-Tamattu or Hajj al-Qiran, not to follow the correct sequence of rites on the 10th of Dhul Hijjah. The correct sequence is: Rami of Jamarah al-Aqaba (the big pillar), then animal sacrifice (Hady) and then trim / shave the hair.	Damm
To delay the slaughter of the animal until after sunset on the 12th of Dhul Hijjah.	Damm
To trim / shave the hair outside the boundaries of the Haram.	Damm
To delay the cutting of the hair until after sunset on the 12th of Dhul Hijjah without a valid reason.	Damm

Day of Arafat

To leave the boundary of Arafat for Muzdalfah before sunset on the 9th of Dhul Hijjah. If the person returns after sunset, the penalty will remain. Penalty is waived if the person returns to Arafat before sunset.	Damm

To proceed directly from Arafat to Mina without performing Wuquf in Muzdalfah, with no valid reason.	Damm

Night of Muzdalfah

To arrive at Muzdalfah on the morning 10th of Dhul Hijjahh after sunrise, with no valid reason.	Damm
To leave Muzdalfah on the 10th of Dhul Hijjahh before Fajr begins, with no valid reason. Penalty is waived if the person returns to Muzdalfah before Fajr. If the person returns after Fajr, the penalty will remain.	Damm

Rami

- ❖ If pelting that was meant to be performed on the 11th or 12th of Dhul Hijjah is omitted, it should be performed on the 12th and 13th instead although the penalty will still be applicable.
- ❖ If the order of pelting on the 11th, 12th and 13th is not followed, no penalty will be due although doing so is against the Sunnah.
- ❖ If the total value of Sadaqah is equivalent to the value of a Damm, slightly less Sadaqah should be given.
- ❖ An elderly, infirm or incapacitated person can appoint someone to pelt on their behalf without incurring any penalties.

- ❖ The person that is appointed to deputise must also remember to carry out their own pelting otherwise a penalty will be incurred by them.

To omit pelting for one day or more.	Damm
To omit up to three pebbles when pelting the Jamarah al-Aqaba on the 10th of Dhul Hijjah.	Sadaqah al-Fitr for each pebble
To omit up to 10 pebbles on the 11th, 12th or 13th Dhul Hijjah. If two or three Jamarat are omitted on these days, Damm is due.	Sadaqah al-Fitr for each pebble
To omit pelting of an entire Jamarat on the 11th, 12th or 13th Dhul Hijjah.	Sadaqah al-Fitr for seven pebbles
To perform Hady before pelting on the 10th of Dhul Hijjah.	Damm
To miss out pelting altogether on this day will result in a Damm	Damm
To pelt on behalf of another person without a valid excuse. Damm is incurred by the person on whose behalf the pelting is carried out for. Only one Damm is due even if it was carried out on three to four days.	Damm
To pelt after sunset on the 13th Dhul Hijjah.	Damm

VIOLATION OF THE HARAM

Hunting

- ❖ Due to its sanctity, it is prohibited to hunt in the Haram, whether in Ihram or not.
- ❖ It is prohibited for someone in Ihram to hunt an animal whether it is in the Haram or outside the Haram.
- ❖ If a person in Ihram kills an animal or aids someone else in killing an animal, a penalty is due. The penalty for killing a prohibited animal within the boundary of the Haram, (whether by a Muhrim or not), is either:
    - To sacrifice a similar animal or an animal similar in size to the animal that was killed, the meat of which should be distributed within the Haram boundary. For example, if a deer was killed, a sheep must be slaughtered. The size or value of such an injured or killed animal is to be determined by two pious Muslims.
    - To attach a value to the animal killed and buy food with this money, distributing it as charity (Sadaqah) for the poor. Sadaqah can be given to anyone and is not restricted to those within the boundaries of the Haram.

- To fast in substitution of the Sadaqah.
- ❖ If a person in Ihram slaughters game, then the slaughtered animal is Maytah (carrion) and is not permissible to consume.
- ❖ Whoever harms an animal, or plucks its feathers, or cuts off one of its limbs, is responsible for that amount which he reduced from its value.
- ❖ Whoever harms an animal resulting in it becoming incapacitated, is responsible for its price in full.
- ❖ There is no penalty for killing animals such as crows, wolves, snakes, scorpions or rats.
- ❖ There is no penalty for killing gnats, mosquitos and ticks.
- ❖ Whoever kills a louse or locust can give as much Sadaqah as he wants.
- ❖ If a predatory animal attacks a Muhrim, who in turn kills the animal, no penalty is due.
- ❖ There is no penalty for eating game which was slaughtered by someone not in Ihram, provided that the person in Ihram did not aid in the killing of the animal.
- ❖ Fishing is permissible in Ihram.

Cutting Vegetation

- ❖ It is prohibited to cut vegetation including trees and grass in the Haram, whether in Ihram or not, due to its sanctity.
- ❖ It is not permissible to cut certain types of vegetation that aren't generally known such as acacia, regardless of whether the land on which it grows is owned by you or not.
- ❖ It is not permissible to allow animals to graze on the grass in the boundaries of the Haram.
- ❖ It is permissible to cut dead trees. It is not permissible to make Miswaak from "wet" trees.
- ❖ It is permissible to cut vegetation that is generally sown such as wheat and barley.
- ❖ The penalty is due immediately after the vegetation has been cut.

SUPPLICATIONS

Supplicate to Allah ﷻ as much as you can. You will be tired of begging but He will not be tired of giving.

Before starting the journey

Perform two Ráka prayers, recite Surah al-Kafiroon in the first and Surah al-Ikhlaas in the second Ráka.

Then, recite the following supplications:

اَللّٰهُمَّ بِكَ اُحَاوِلُ وَبِكَ اُصَاوِلُ وَبِكَ اَسِيْرُ

(O Allah! I move by your aid and I attack by your aid and I make captive by Your aid)

يَا كَرِيْمُ يَا رَحِيْمُ يَا حَفِيْظُ يَا سَلَامُ

(Ya Kareemu, Ya Raheemu, Ya Hafeezu, Ya Salamu)
Three times

اللّٰهُ حَفِيْظٌ لَطِيْفٌ قَدِيْمٌ اَزَلِيٌّ حَيٌّ الْقَيُّوْمُ لَا يَنَامُ

(Allahu Hafeezu, Lateefu, Qadeemu, Azaliyo, Hayyu, Qayum, La Yanamu) -Seven times

Recite '**Ya** Raqeebu' 117 times. Write seven times on your baggage, with your finger:

يَا رَقِيْبُ

(Ya Raqeebu) 117 times

Recite the following seven times:

وَاللّٰهُ مِنْ وَّرَآئِهِمْ مُحِيْطٌ

(And Allah has embraced them all around)

بِسْمِ اللّٰهِ وَاعْتَصَمْتُ بِاللّٰهِ وَتَوَكَّلْتُ عَلَى اللّٰهِ وَلَا اِلٰهَ اِلَّا اللّٰهُ وَاللّٰهُ اَكْبَر

(In the name of Allah and I hold on to Allah firmly and I trust in Allah and there is no one worthy of being worshipped other than Allah and Allah is the Greatest)

Recite Surah al-Fatiha three times, then recite the following supplication:

اَللّٰهُمَّ سَلِّمْنِىْ وَسَلِّمْ مَا مَعِىْ وَاحْفَظْنِىْ وَاحْفَظْ مَا مَعِىْ وَبَلِّغْنِىْ وَبَلِّغْ مَا مَعِىْ

(O Allah! Protect me and my belongings and safeguard my belongings and take me (to the destination) with my belongings)

Recite Ayat al-Kursi three times and recite:

اَللّٰهُمَّ سَلِّمْنِىْ وَسَلِّمْ مَا مَعِىْ وَاحْفَظْنِىْ وَاحْفَظْ مَا مَعِىْ وَبَلِّغْنِىْ وَبَلِّغْ مَا مَعِىْ

(O Allah! Protect me and my belongings and safeguard my belongings and take me (to the destination) with my belongings)

Recite Surah al-Qadr three times and then recite:

اَللّٰهُمَّ سَلِّمْنِىْ وَسَلِّمْ مَا مَعِىْ وَاحْفَظْنِىْ وَاحْفَظْ مَا مَعِىْ وَبَلِّغْنِىْ وَبَلِّغْ مَا مَعِىْ

(O Allah! Protect me and my belongings and safeguard my belongings and take me (to the destination) with my belongings)

Read the following supplication:

اَللّٰهُمَّ اِنَّا نَسْئَلُكَ فِىْ سَفَرِنَا هٰذَا الْبِرَّ وَالتَّقْوٰى وَالْعَمَلَ مَا تَرْضٰى

اَللّٰهُمَّ هَوِّنْ عَلَيْنَا سَفَرَنَا هٰذَا وَاطْوِ عَنَّا بُعْدَهٗ، اَللّٰهُمَّ اَنْتَ الصَّاحِبُ فِى السَّفَرِ وَالْخَلِيْفَةُ فِى الْاَهْلِ

اَللّٰهُمَّ اِنِّىْ اَعُوْذُبِكَ مِنْ وَعْثَاءِ السَّفَرِ وَكَآبَةِ الْمَنْظَرِ وَسُوْءِ الْمُنْقَلَبِ فِى الْمَالِ وَالْاَهْلِ

وَالْوَلَدِ وَ اَعُوْذُبِكَ مِنَ الْحَوْرِ بَعْدَ الْكَوْرِ وَدَعْوَةِ الْمَظْلُوْمِ

*(O Allah! We seek the provisions of piety and devotion.
And seek Your Grace to act in accordance with Your liking.
Allah! Make this journey easy and reduce its span.
Allah! You are our Companion in this journey and the
Protector of our families.
Allah! We seek refuge in You from the fatigue of this
journey, from sorrowful scenes and a return where there is a
loss or deficiency to family or wealth)*

Recite the following supplication once before leaving the house, then recite it during the journey. Inshá Allah, Allah will give the opportunity to visit Makkah and Madinah again.

إِنَّ الَّذِي فَرَضَ عَلَيْكَ الْقُرْآنَ لَرَآدُّكَ إِلَى مَعَادٍ

[Most certainly, the One Who has ordained the Quran for you will "ultimately" bring you back home] [Qurán, al Qasas 28,85]

Upon leaving the house

بِسْمِ اللهِ تَوَكَّلْتُ عَلَى اللهِ لَاحَوْلَ وَلَا قُوَّةَ إِلَّا بِاللهِ

(In the name of Allah, I trust in Allah, there is no power nor strength except by Allah the Lofty, the Great)

Look at the sky and recite:

اللَّهُمَّ إِنِّي أَعُوذُ بِكَ مِنْ أَنْ أَضِلَّ أَوْ أُضَلَّ أَوْ أَزِلَّ أَوْ أُزَلَّ أَوْ أَظْلِمَ أَوْ أُظْلَمَ أَوْ أَجْهَلَ أَوْ يُجْهَلَ عَلَيَّ

(O Allah! I seek refuge in You from being astray myself or by someone, or I error (from the right path) myself or by someone, or I oppress someone or I am oppressed, or I behave ignorantly or being treated ill)

Upon riding your vehicle

سُبْحَانَ الَّذِي سَخَّرَ لَنَا هَذَا وَمَا كُنَّا لَهُ مُقْرِنِينَ وَإِنَّا إِلَى رَبِّنَا لَمُنْقَلِبُونَ

(In the name of Allah, and Praise be to Allah. Glory be to the One who has placed this (transport) at our service and we ourselves would not have been capable of that, and to our Lord we will surely return)

Then, recite the following three times each:

الحَمْدُلِلَّه *(Alhumdolillah),* اللهُ اَكْبَر *(Allahu Akbar),* لَاإِلٰهَ إِلَّا اللهُ *(La ilaha Illalah)*

سُبْحَانَكَ إِنِّي ظَلَمْتُ نَفْسِي ظُلْمًا كَثِيرًا وَأَنَا غْفِرْ لِي فَإِنَّهُ لَا يَغْفِرُ الذُّنُوبَ إِلَّا أَنْتَ

(O Allah! I have considerably wronged myself. There is none to forgive the sins but You. So, grant me pardon and

have mercy on me. You are the Most Forgiving, the Most Compassionate.)

It is Sunnah to smile upon reciting this supplication. Keep reciting the following Surahs during the journey. Recite Bismillah before every Surah and at the end, recite Bismillah one more time.

Surah al-Kafiroon, Surah an-Nasr, Surah al-Ikhlaas, Surah al-Falq, Surah al-Nas

Upon feeling anxious

سُبْحَانَ الْمَلِكِ الْقُدُّوسِ رَبِّ الْمَلٰئِكَةِ وَالرُّوحِ جَنَّاتِ السَّمٰوٰتِ بِالْعِزَّةِ وَالْجَبَرُوْتِ

(Glory be to Allah, Beyond being conditioned is the Sublime King, the Master of the angels and Gibrael, the One who is venerated in the skies, the Venerable, the Magnificent)

Upon reaching the airport, recite:

أَعُوذُ بِكَلِمَاتِ اللهِ التَّامَّاتِ مِنْ شَرِّ مَا خَلَقَ

(I seek refuge in the Perfect Words of Allah from the evil of what He has created)

اَللّٰهُمَّ بَارِكْ لَنَا فِيْهِ

(Allah! Give us barakah in this)

اَللّٰهُمَّ ارْزُقْنَا جَنَاهَا وَحَبِّبْنَا اِلٰی اَهْلِهَا وَحَبِّبْ صَالِحِیْ اَهْلِهَا اِلَیْنَا

(O Allah! Give us fruits as food from this city and make us beloved to the reisdents of this city and make the pious of this city beloved to us)

رَبِّ اَنْزِلْنِیْ مُنْزَلًا مُّبَارَكًا وَّاَنْتَ خَیْرُ الْمُنْزِلِیْنَ

(My Lord! Make me land at a blessed destination and You are the Best of those who bring to destination)

Upon entering Makkah or Madinah

اَللّٰهُمَّ رَبَّ السَّمٰوٰتِ السَّبْعِ وَمَا اَظْلَلْنَ وَرَبَّ الْاَرَضِیْنَ السَّبْعِ وَمَا اَقْلَلْنَ وَرَبَّ الشَّیٰطِیْنِ وَمَا اَضْلَلْنَ وَرَبَّ الرِّیَاحِ وَمَا ذَرَیْنَ فَاِنَّا نَسْئَلُكَ خَیْرَ هٰذِهِ الْقَرْیَةِ وَخَیْرَ اَهْلِهَا وَنَعُوْذُبِكَ مِنْ شَرِّهَا وَشَرِّ اَهْلِهَا وَشَرِّ مَا فِیْهَا

(O Allah! The Lord of the Seven skies and those which they shade! The Lord of the lands and those which they hold! The Lord of shayateen and those which they led astray! The Lord of the winds and those which they spread! Indeed, we seek from You blessings of this dwelling and its residents and seek refuge in You from the evil of this dwelling and its residents.)

Intention for Umrah

اللَّهُمَّ اِنِّى اُرِيْدُ الْعُمْرَةَ فَيَسِّرْهَا لِى وَتَقَبَّلْهَا مِنِّى وَتَقَبَّلْهَا مِنِّى

(O Allah! I make intention to perform Umrah, make it easy for me and accept it)

Then, recite Talbiyah:

لَبَّيْكَ اللَّهُمَّ لَبَّيْكَ لَبَّيْكَ لَا شَرِيْكَ لَكَ لَبَّيْكَ اِنَّ الْحَمْدَ وَالنِّعْمَةَ لَكَ وَالْمُلْكَ لَا شَرِيْكَ لَكَ

(Here I am, O Lord, here I am, You indeed have no partner, here I am. Indeed, all praise and bounties are Yours, and so is the absolute Domain. You indeed have no partners, here I am.)

Supplicate:

اللَّهُمَّ اِنِّى اَسْئَلُكَ رِضَاكَ وَالْجَنَّةَ وَاَعُوْذُ بِكَ مِنْ غَضَبِكَ وَالنَّارِ

(O Allah! I seek Your rida and Jannah and I seek refuge from Your displeasure and Hell.)

Entering the boundaries of Haram

اَللّٰهُمَّ إِنَّ هٰذَا حَرَمُكَ وَحَرَمُ رَسُوْلِكَ، فَحَرِّمْ لَحْمِيْ وَدَمِيْ وَعَظْمِيْ عَلَى النَّارِ اَللّٰهُمَّ اٰمِنِّيْ مِنْ عَذَابِكَ يَوْمَ تَبْعَثُ عِبَادَكَ وَاجْعَلْنِيْ مِنْ أَوْلِيَآئِكَ وَأَهْلِ طَاعَتِكَ وَتُبْ عَلَيَّ إِنَّكَ أَنْتَ التَّوَّابُ الرَّحِيْمُ

(O Allah! This is Your and Your Prophet's ﷺ Haram. Prevent my flesh, blood and bones from the fire. O Allah! Save me from Your torment. Include me amongst Your friends and the pious on the Day of Resurrection and keep me in Your Grace. Indeed, You are the One who accepts repentance and the Most Merciful.)

At the entrance of the Haram

بِسْمِ اللّٰهِ وَالصَّلٰوةُ وَالسَّلَامُ عَلٰى رَسُوْلِ اللّٰهِ اَللّٰهُمَّ اغْفِرْ لِيْ ذُنُوْبِيْ وَافْتَحْ لِيْ أَبْوَابَ رَحْمَتِكَ

(In the name of Allah, all Praises are due to Him, and salutations upon the Messenger of Allah. O Allah! Forgive my sins and open the gates of Your mercy.)

In the middle of the Haram

رَبَّنَا اٰتِنَا فِی الدُّنْیَا حَسَنَۃً وَّفِی الْاٰخِرَۃِ حَسَنَۃً وَّقِنَا عَذَابَ النَّارِ اَللّٰهُمَّ اِنِّیْ اَسْئَلُكَ مِنْ خَیْرِ مَا سَاَلَكَ عَبْدُكَ وَنَبِیُّكَ مُحَمَّدٌ صَلَّی اللّٰهُ عَلَیْهِ وَسَلَّمَ وَاَعُوْذُبِكَ مِنْ شَرِّ مَا اسْتَعَاذَ مِنْهُ عَبْدُكَ وَنَبِیُّكَ

(Our Lord! Grant me the good of this world and the Hereafter and protect me from the torment of fire. O Allah! I beg You the good which Your Prophet Muhammad ﷺ begged of You; and I seek refuge in You from the evil from which the Prophet Muhammad ﷺ sought refuge.)

Intention of I'itikaaf

نَوَیْتُ الْاِعْتِكَافَ مَا دُمْتُ فِیْ هٰذَا الْمَسْجِدِ

(I make the intention of I'tikaaf till I am in this Masjid)

At the first sight upon Kaába

اَللّٰهُ اَكْبَرُ اللّٰهُ اَكْبَرُ لِلّٰهِ اَكْبَرُ لَا اِلٰهَ اِلَّا اللّٰهُ لَا اِلٰهَ اِلَّا اللّٰهُ وَاللّٰهُ اَكْبَرُ

(Allah is the Greatest, Allah is the Greatest, Allah is the Greatest, there is no Lord except for Allah, there is no Lord except for Allah and Allah is the Greatest.)

Intention for circumambulation (Tawaf) for Umrah

اَللّٰهُمَّ اِنِّیْ اُرِیْدُ طَوَافَ بَیْتِکَ الْحَرَامِ فَیَسِّرْہُ لِیْ وَتَقَبَّلْهُ مِنِّیْ سَبْعَةَ اَشْوَاطٍ لِلّٰهِ تَعَالٰی عَزَّ وَجَلَّ

(O Allah! I make the intention of Tawaf, make it easy for me and accept the seven circuits)

Intention for Tawaf al-Nafl

اَللّٰهُمَّ اِنِّیْ اُرِیْدُ طَوَافَ بَیْتِکَ الْمُحَرَّمِ فَیَسِّرْہُ لِیْ وَتَقَبَّلْهُ مِنِّیْ

(O Allah! I make the intention of Tawaf, make it easy for me and accept it)

Standing in front of the Hajr e Aswad

بِسْمِ اللهِ اللهُ اَکْبَرُ لَااِلٰہَ اِلَّا اللهُ وَلِلّٰہِ الْحَمْدُ وَالصَّلٰوةُ وَالسَّلَامُ عَلٰی رَسُوْلِ اللهِ اَللّٰهُمَّ اِیْمَانًا بِکَ وَوَفَاءً بِعَهْدِکَ وَاتِّبَاعًا لِّسُنَّةِ نَبِیِّکَ مُحَمَّدٍ صَلَّی اللهُ عَلَیْهِ وَآلِهٖ وَسَلَّمَ

(In the name of Allah, Allah the Greatest; There is no Lord except for Allah and all praises are due to Allah and supplications upon Allah's Messenger ﷺ. O Allah! By the belief in You and in accordance with Your command and

abiding by the promise and in accordance with the Sunnah of the Prophet Muhammad ﷺ.)

Between Hajr e Aswad and Rukn e Shami, (first to third corner)

سُبْحَانَ اللهِ وَالْحَمْدُ لِلّٰهِ وَلَا اِلٰهَ اِلَّا اللّٰهُ وَاللهُ اَكْبَرُ وَلَا حَوْلَ وَلَا قُوَّةَ اِلَّا بِاللهِ الْعَلِيِّ الْعَظِيْمِ

(Glory be to Allah and praise be to Allah, and there is none worthy of worship but Allah, and Allah is the Greatest. And there is no might or power except with Allah, the Exalted, the Great)

Between Rukn e Shami and Rukn e Yemeni (Third to fourth corner)

اَللّٰهُمَّ اِنِّيْ اَعُوْذُبِكَ مِنَ الشِّرْكِ وَالشَّكِّ وَالنِّفَاقِ وَالشِّقَاقِ وَسُوْءِ الْاَخْلَاقِ وَسُوْءِ الْمُنْقَلَبِ فِي الْمَالِ وَالْاَهْلِ وَالْوَلَدِ

(O Allah! I seek refuge in You from shirk, doubt, hypocrisy, divergence, insolent conduct and bad turning of wealth, family and children)

اَللّٰهُمَّ اِنِّىْ اَسْئَلُكَ الرَّاحَةَ عِنْدَ الْمَوْتِ وَالْعَفْوَ عِنْدَ الْحِسَابِ

(O Allah! I seek Your solace at the time of death and mercy at the time of Judgement)

اَللّٰهُمَّ اِنِّىْ اَسْئَلُكَ رِضَاكَ وَالْجَنَّةَ وَاَعُوْذُبِكَ مِنْ غَضَبِكَ وَالنَّارِ

(O Allah! I seek Your rida and Jannah and I seek refuge in You from Your displeasure and Hellfire)

Between Rukn e Yemeni and Hajr e Aswad (fourth to first corner)

اَللّٰهُمَّ اِنِّىْ اَسْئَلُكَ الْعَفْوَ وَالْعَافِيَةَ فِى الدُّنْيَا وَالْاٰخِرَةِ رَبَّنَا اٰتِنَا فِى الدُّنْيَا حَسَنَةً وَّفِى الْاٰخِرَةِ حَسَنَةً وَّقِنَا عَذَابَ النَّارِ

(O Allah! I seek mercy and to be save from affliction in this world and hereafter. O Allah! Grant us good in this world and the hereafter and save us from the torment of fire)

اَللّٰهُمَّ اِنِّىْ اَعُوْذُبِكَ مِنَ الْكُفْرِ وَالْفَاقَةِ وَمَوَاقِىْ فِى الدُّنْيَا وَالْاٰخِرَةِ

At Multazam

اللَّهُمَّ رَبَّ الْبَيْتِ الْعَتِيقِ اَعْتِقْ رِقَابَنَا وَرِقَابَ اٰبَائِنَا وَاُمَّهَاتِنَا وَاِخْوَانِنَا وَاَوْلَادِنَا مِنَ النَّارِ

يَاذَا الْجُوْدِ وَالْكَرَمِ وَالْفَضْلِ وَالْمَنِّ وَالْعَطَاءِ وَالْاِحْسَانِ

اللَّهُمَّ اَحْسِنْ عَاقِبَتَنَا فِي الْاُمُوْرِ كُلِّهَا وَاَجِرْنَا مِنْ خِزْيِ الدُّنْيَا وَعَذَابِ الْاٰخِرَةِ

اللَّهُمَّ اِنِّي عَبْدُكَ وَبْنُ عَبْدِكَ وَاقِفٌ تَحْتَ بَابِكَ مُلْتَزِمٌ بِاَعْتَابِكَ مُتَذَلِّلٌ بَيْنَ يَدَيْكَ، اَرْجُوْ رَحْمَتَكَ وَاَخْشٰى عَذَابَكَ يَاقَدِيْمَ الْاِحْسَانِ

اللَّهُمَّ اِنِّي اَسْاَلُكَ اَنْ تَرْفَعَ ذِكْرِي وَتَضَعَ وِزْرِي وَتُصْلِحَ اَمْرِيْ وَتُطَهِّرَ قَلْبِي، وَتُنَوِّرَ لِي قَلْبِي وَتَغْفِرَ لِي ذَنْبِي وَاَسْاَلُكَ الدَّرَجَاتِ الْعُلٰى مِنَ الْجَنَّةِ

اللَّهُمَّ ارْزُقْنِي شَهَادَةً فِي سَبِيْلِكَ وَاجْعَلْ مَوْتِي فِي بَلَدِ رَسُوْلِكَ

(O Allah, the Owner of this ancient House! Save our necks and the necks of our ancestors, mothers, brothers and children from the Hellfire.

O the Merciful, the Gracious, the Virtuous, the Benevolent, the Generous, O Allah! Bless us in all matters, save us from disgrace in this world and the torment in the hereafter.

O Allah! I am Your slave and the son of Your slave, standing at Your door and standing close to Your door, I beg Your mercy and afraid of the torment of the Hell.

O Allah! Make my mention better and ease the burden of my sins and improve my matters and cleanse my heart and enlighten my grave and forgive my sins and I seek the higher levels of Jannah from You)

(O Allah! Grant me martyrdom in your way and appoint my death in the city of the Prophet ﷺ)

At Maqam e Ibraheem

وَاتَّخِذُوْا مِنْ مَّقَامِ إِبْرٰهِيْمَ مُصَلًّى

(And take the standing place of Abraham as a site for prayer)

Upon drinking Zamzam

اللّٰهُمَّ إِنِّيْ أَسْأَلُكَ عِلْمًا نَافِعًا وَرِزْقًا وَاسِعًا وَشِفَاءً مِنْ كُلِّ دَاءٍ

(O Allah! I seek plentiful sustenance, beneficial knowledge and cure from every disease)

Upon leaving from Baab al-Safa

بِسْمِ اللهِ وَالصَّلَاةُ وَالسَّلَامُ عَلَى رَسُوْلِ اللهِ رَبِّ اغْفِرْ لِيْ ذُنُوْبِيْ وَافْتَحْ لِيْ أَبْوَابَ فَضْلِكَ

(In the name of Allah and benediction upon Allah's Prophet ﷺ. O Lord! Forgive my sins and open the doors of Your Grace upon me)

Walking towards the Mount of Safa

إِنِّيْ أَبْدَأُ بِمَا بَدَأَ اللهُ بِهِ إِنَّ الصَّفَا وَالْمَرْوَةَ مِنْ شَعَائِرِ اللهِ

(Indeed, I begin with which Allah did. Indeed, Safa and Marwa are signs of Allah)

Intention to make Saé

(O Allah! I intend to make the seven circuits of S of Safa and Marwa for (Hajj or Umrah). Make it easy for me and accept it)

Then, raise hands as in supplication and say Allahu Akbar three times, then recite the fourth Kalima, as follows:

$$\text{لَا إِلٰهَ إِلَّا اللهُ وَحْدَهُ لَا شَرِيكَ لَهُ لَهُ الْمُلْكُ وَلَهُ الْحَمْدُ يُحْيِي وَيُمِيتُ بِيَدِهِ الْخَيْرُ وَهُوَ عَلَىٰ كُلِّ شَيْءٍ قَدِيرٌ}$$

(There is none worthy of worship besides Allah, He has no partners, for Him is the kingdom and all praise, He is the giver of life and death, in His decree is all good and His power rules over everything)

At Safa

$$\text{اللّٰهُمَّ إِنَّكَ قُلْتَ ادْعُونِي أَسْتَجِبْ لَكُمْ وَإِنَّكَ لَا تُخْلِفُ الْمِيعَادَ وَإِنِّي أَسْأَلُكَ كَمَا هَدَيْتَنِي لِلْإِسْلَامِ أَنْ لَا تَنْزِعَهُ مِنِّي حَتّٰى تَتَوَفَّانِي وَأَنَا مُسْلِمٌ}$$

(O Allah! You commanded, 'Seek and I will accept', and You do not break promise, indeed, I seek that You granted me guidance through Islam, so do not take it away from me and give me death in the state of Islam)

While walking towards Marwa, recite the fourth Kalima. Between the green pillars, recite:

$$\text{رَبِّ اغْفِرْ وَارْحَمْ إِنَّكَ أَنْتَ الْأَعَزُّ الْأَكْرَمُ}$$

(O Lord! Forgive and have mercy, indeed You are the Venerable, the Generous)

Hajj

Intention for Hajj

اَللَّهُمَّ إِنِّي أُرِيْدُ الْحَجَّ فَيَسِّرْهُ لِيْ وَ تَقَبَّلْهُ مِنِّي

(O Allah! I make the intention for Hajj. Make it easy for me and accept it)

From the Fajr of 9th Dhul Hijjah to Asar of 13th Dhul Hijjah

اَللهُ اَكْبَرُ اللهُ اَكْبَرُ لَا اِلٰهَ اِلَّا اللهُ وَاللهُ اَكْبَرُ اللهُ اَكْبَرُ وَلِلهِ الْحَمْدُ

(Allah is the Greatest, Allah is the Greatest, there is none worthy of worship except for Allah, and Allah is the Greatest, Allah is the Greatest and all praises are to Him)

Recite Surah al-Kahf at Safa and again at Marwa

While in Arafat

Recite, Fourth Kalima-100 times, Durood Ibraheemi-100 times, Surah al-Ikhlaas-100 times and Istighfar-100 times.

اَللّٰهُمَّ صَلِّ عَلٰى مُحَمَّدٍ وَّعَلٰى آلِ مُحَمَّدٍ كَمَا صَلَّيْتَ عَلٰى إِبْرَاهِيْمَ وَعَلٰى آلِ إِبْرَاهِيْمَ إِنَّكَ حَمِيْدٌ مَّجِيْدٌ

(O Allah! send peace upon Prophet Muhammad ﷺ and to the family of Prophet Muhammad ﷺ as you sent peace on Prophet Ibrahim ﷺ and the family of Prophet Ibrahim ﷺ. Indeed, You are Praiseworthy and Glorious. O Allah! Bless the Prophet Muhammad ﷺ and the family of Prophet Muhammad ﷺ as you blessed Prophet Ibrahim ﷺ and the family of Prophet Ibrahim ﷺ. Indeed, You are Praiseworthy and Glorious)

أَسْتَغْفِرُ اللهَ الَّذِىْ لَآ اِلٰهَ اِلَّا هُوَ الْحَىُّ الْقَيُّوْمُ وَأَتُوْبُ إِلَيْهِ

(I seek forgiveness of Allah, the Almighty, there is none worthy of worship except Him, the Living, the eternal, and I repent to Him)

After the fourth Kalima, recite:

اَللّٰهُمَّ اجْعَلْ فِىْ قَلْبِىْ نُوْرًا وَّفِىْ سَمْعِىْ نُوْرًا وَّفِىْ بَصَرِىْ نُوْرًا

(O Allah! Illuminate my heart and illuminate my eyes and illuminate my ears)

اَللّٰهُمَّ اشْرَحْ لِىْ صَدْرِىْ وَيَسِّرْ لِىْ أَمْرِىْ وَأَعُوْذُبِكَ مِنْ وَسَاوِسِ الصَّدْرِ وَشَتَّاتِ الْأَمْرِ وَفِتْنَةِ الْقَبْرِ

(O Allah! Expand my chest, and make my matters easy and I seek refuge in You from the evil doubts of my heart, transgression of matters and the trial of grave)

اَللّٰهُمَّ اِنِّیْ اَعُوْذُبِكَ مِنْ شَرِّ مَا یَلِجُ فِی اللَّیْلِ وَ شَرِّ مَا یَلِجُ فِی النَّهَارِ وَ شَرِّ مَا تَهَبُّ بِهِ الرِّیَاحُ

(O Allah! I seek refuge in You from the evil of that which enters through the night and the evil of that which enters through the day and the evil of that which is carried by the wind)

Upon picking the pebbles at Muzdalfa

Supplicate to Allah in your own words and also recite:

(O Allah! You are above any defects and flaws. We are humans and we have erred. We have sinned and oppressed many. You are Merciful and Gracious, forgive our sins and recompense the oppressed)

Upon casting pebbles at Shaytan

بِسْمِ اللهِ اللهُ اَكْبَرُ وَغَمَّا لِلشَّیْطَانِ وَرِضَی الرَّحْمٰنِ اللّٰهُمَّ اجْعَلْهُ حَجًّا مَبْرُوْراً وُسَعْیَهَا مَشْكُوْراً وَذَنْبًا مَغْفُوْراً

(In the name of Allah, Allah is the Greatest. To submit Shaytan and to please the Rahman(Allah). O Allah! Accept this Hajj and accept my endeavour and make it a source of deliverance from my sins)

Supplications in Madinah-The Radiant

Upon the first sight of Madinah

Send blessings upon the Beloved Prophet ﷺ and recite:

اَللّٰهُمَّ هٰذَا اَحْرَمُ نَبِيِّكَ فَاجْعَلْهُ وَقَايَةً مِّنَ النَّارِ وَ اَمَانًا مِّنَ الْعَذَابِ وَ سُوْءِ الْحِسَابِ

(O Allah! This is the house of Your Prophet ﷺ, so protect it from fire and grant it peace from torment and the time of Judgement)

Upon entering the Masjid al-Nabawi

بِسْمِ اللّٰهِ وَالصَّلٰوةُ وَالسَّلَامُ عَلٰى رَسُوْلِ اللّٰهِ رَبِّ اغْفِرْلِيْ ذُنُوْبِيْ وَافْتَحْ لِيْ اَبْوَابَ رَحْمَتِكَ

(In the name of Allah and benediction upon Allah's Prophet ﷺ. O Lord! Forgive my sins and open the doors of Your Grace upon me)

Send Blessings upon the Beloved Prophet ﷺ

السَّلَامُ عَلَيْكَ يَا رَسُولَ اللهِ السَّلَامُ عَلَيْكَ يَا حَبِيْبَ اللهِ

السَّلَامُ عَلَيْكَ يَا نَبِيَّ اللهِ السَّلَامُ عَلَيْكَ اَيُّهَا النَّبِيُّ وَرَحْمَةُ اللهِ وَبَرَكَاتُهُ

اَلصَّلٰوةُ وَالسَّلَامُ عَلَيْكَ يَا رَسُولَ اللهِ

(Assalam o alaika O Allah's Messenger ﷺ, Assalam o Alaika O Allah's Beloved ﷺ, Assalam o Alaika O Allah's Prophet ﷺ, O Prophet ﷺ! Allah's blessings and Grace be upon you. O Allah's Messenger ﷺ! Peace and blessings be upon you)

In front of the Sacred Rawdah

اِنَّ اللهَ وَمَلٰٓئِكَتَهٗ يُصَلُّوْنَ عَلَى النَّبِيِّ يٰٓاَيُّهَا الَّذِيْنَ اٰمَنُوْا صَلُّوْا عَلَيْهِ وَسَلِّمُوْا تَسْلِيْمًا

(Indeed, Allah showers His blessings upon the Prophet ﷺ, and His angels pray for him. O believers! Invoke Allah's blessings upon him, and salute him with worthy greetings of peace)

Then, send the blessings at least seventy times:

صَلَّى اللهُ عَلَيْكَ يَا رَسُولَ اللهِ

(O Allah's Messenger ﷺ! Peace be upon you)

Then, supplicate:

اَللَّهُمَّ اِنَّكَ قُلْتَ فِيْ كِتَابِكَ لِنَبِيِّكَ عَلَيْهِ السَّلَامُ وَلَوْ اَنَّهُمْ اِذْظَلَمُوْا اَنْفُسَهُمْ جَآءُوْكَ فَاسْتَغْفَرُوا اللّٰهَ وَاسْتَغْفَرَ لَهُمُ الرَّسُوْلُ لَوَجَدُوا اللّٰهَ تَوَّابًا رَحِيْمًا وَاِنِّيْ قَدْ اَتَيْتُ نَبِيَّكَ مُسْتَغْفِرًا فَاَسْئَلُكَ اَنْ تُوْجِبَ لِيَ الْمَغْفِرَةَ كَمَا اَوْجَبْتَهَا لِمَنْ اَتَاهُ فِيْ حَيَاتِهِ اَللّٰهُمَّ اِنِّيْ اَتَوَجَّهُ اِلَيْكَ بِنَبِيِّكَ صَلَّى اللّٰهُ عَلَيْهِ وَسَلَّمَ۔

(O Allah! You have mentioned in the Book (Qurán) to the Prophet ﷺ, "If only those came to you—after wronging themselves—seeking Allah's forgiveness and the Messenger ﷺ prayed for their forgiveness, they would have certainly found Allah ever Accepting of Repentance, Most Merciful." [al Nisa, 4:64]. Indeed, I have come to Allah's Prophet ﷺ seeking forgiveness, therefore forgive me as You forgave those who came to the Beloved Prophet ﷺ in his life. O Allah! I stand before the Prophet ﷺ.)

Also supplicate in these words:

(O Allah! Your Prophet ﷺ is Your beloved,, Shaytan is your enemy and I am Your slave. If you forgive me, Your Beloved ﷺ would be pleased, Your enemy will be displeased and Your slave will be saved. If You do not forgive me, Your Beloved ﷺ would be sad, Your enemy will be happy and Your slave will be doomed.

O Allah! It was a tradition amongst the nobles of Arab to free slaves on the graves of their chiefs. This is the resting place of the chief of the worlds. Your command is to free the slaves, so, forgive me and grant me deliverance from hellfire)

Sending blessings from someone else

اَلسَّلَامُ عَلَيْكَ يَا رَسُوْلَ اللّٰهِ مِنْ (the name of the person)

يَسْتَشْفِعُ بِكَ اِلٰى رَبِّكَ

Sending blessings from many people

اَلسَّلَامُ عَلَيْكَ يَا رَسُوْلَ اللّٰهِ مِنْ جَمِيْعِ مَنْ اَوْصَانِىْ بِالسَّلَامِ عَلَيْكَ

(Assalam o Alaika Allah's Messenger ﷺ, from all those who asked me to present their salam)

Blessings upon Sayeddina Abu Bakr Siddique ﷺ

اَلسَّلَامُ عَلَيْكَ يَا خَلِيْفَةَ رَسُوْلِ اللّٰهِ اَلسَّلَامُ عَلَيْكَ يَا اَبَا بَكْرِ الصِّدِّيْقِ

رَضِىَ اللّٰهُ عَنْهُ

(Assalam o Alaika, O Caliph of Allah's Messenger ﷺ, Assalam o Alaika O Abu Bakr Siddique ﷺ)

Blessings upon Sayeddina Umar ﷺ

اَلسَّلَامُ عَلَيْكَ يَا اَمِيْرُ الْمُؤْمِنِيْنَ اَلسَّلَامُ عَلَيْكَ عُمَرَ الْفَارُوْقِ رَضِىَ اللهُ تَعَالٰى عَنْهُ

(Assalam o Alayka O Leader of the Faithful, Assalam o Alayka Umar al-Farooque ﷺ)

Blessings to Sayeddina Abu Bakr Siddique ﷺ and Sayeddina Umar ﷺ

اَلسَّلَامُ عَلَيْكُمَا يَا ضَجِيْعَىْ رَسُوْلِ اللهِ وَ وَزِيْرَيْهِ جَزَاكُمَا اللهُ اَحْسَنَ الْجَزَآءِ جِئْنَاكُمَا نَتَوَسَّلُ بِكُمْ اِلٰى رَسُوْلِ اللهِ صَلَّى اللهُ عَلَيْهِ وَسَلَّمَ لِيَشْفَعَ لَنَا وَ يَدْعُوْ لَنَا رَبَّنَا اَنْ يُّحْيِيَنَا عَلٰى مِلَّتِهِ وَ سُنَّتِهِ وَ يَحْشُرَنَا فِىْ زُمْرَتِهِ وَ جَمِيْعِ الْمُسْلِمِيْنَ

(Peace be upon the ones lying next to Allah's Messenger ﷺ, the two Viziers. May Allah recompense you. We seek your intercession to the Beloved Prophet ﷺ to supplicate to Allah to keep us firm on Islam and count us amongst the followers of the Beloved Prophet ﷺ on the Day of Judgement)

Upon visiting Jannat al-Baqeé

اَلسَّلَامُ عَلَيْكَ يَا اَهْلَ الْبَقِيْعِ

(Assalam o alaika, O dwellers of Baqée)

During the return journey

لَاإِلٰهَ إِلَّا اللّٰهُ وَحْدَهُ لَاشَرِيْكَ لَهُ لَهُ الْمُلْكُ وَلَهُ الْحَمْدُ يُحْيِىْ وَيُمِيْتُ بِيَدِهِ الْخَيْرُ وَهُوَ عَلٰى كُلِّ شَيْءٍ قَدِيْرٌ

(There is none worthy of worship besides Allah, He has no partners, for Him is the kingdom and all praise, He is the giver of life and death, in His decree is all good and His power rules over everything)

آئِبُوْنَ تَائِبُوْنَ عَابِدُوْنَ سَاجِدُوْنَ سَائِحُوْنَ لِرَبِّنَا حَامِدُوْنَ ـ صَدَقَ اللّٰهُ وَعْدَهُ وَنَصَرَ عَبْدَهُ وَهَزَمَ الْاَحْزَابَ وَحْدَهُ

(We are the returning, penitent, devotees who prostrate before You, the ones who fast, the ones who praise the Lord. Allah has fulfilled His promise and helped His servant (Allah's Messenger ﷺ) and he conquered the troops (enemies) alone)

Upon reaching hometown

آئِبُوْنَ تَائِبُوْنَ عَابِدُوْنَ لِرَبِّنَا حَامِدُوْنَ

(We are the returning, penitent, devotees who praise the Lord)

Upon reaching Home

اَوْباً اَوْباً لِرَبِّنَا تَوْباً لَا يُغَادِرُ عَلَيْنَا حَوْباً۔

(We return and we return penitent and beseeching that all our sins be absolved)

Notes

www.ingramcontent.com/pod-product-compliance
Lightning Source LLC
Chambersburg PA
CBHW030258010526
44107CB00053B/1755